EARLIER AMERICAN MUSIC

EDITED BY H. WILEY HITCHCOCK

for the *Music Library Association*

6

THE HARMONY OF MAINE

THE HARMONY OF MAINE

BY SUPPLY BELCHER

NEW INTRODUCTION BY H. WILEY HITCHCOCK
Director, Institute for Studies in American Music,
Brooklyn College, CUNY

DA CAPO PRESS • NEW YORK • 1972

This Da Capo Press edition of *The Harmony of Maine*
is an unabridged republication of the first edition
published in 1794.

Library of Congress Catalog Card Number 77-169607
ISBN 0-306-77306-6

Published by Da Capo Press, Inc.
A Subsidiary of Plenum Publishing Corporation
227 West 17th Street, New York, New York 10011

Manufactured in the United States of America

EDITOR'S FOREWORD

American musical culture, from Colonial and Federal Era days on, has been reflected in an astonishing production of printed music of all kinds: by 1820, for instance, more than fifteen thousand musical publications had issued from American presses. Fads, fashions, and tastes have changed so rapidly in our history, however, that comparatively little earlier American music has remained in print. On the other hand, the past few decades have seen an explosion of interest in earlier American culture, including earlier American music. College and university courses in American civilization and American music have proliferated; recording companies have found a surprising response to earlier American composers and their music; a wave of interest in folk and popular music of past eras has opened up byways of musical experience unimagined only a short time ago.

It seems an opportune moment, therefore, to make available for study and enjoyment—and as an aid to furthering performance of earlier American music—works of significance that exist today only in a few scattered copies of publications long out of print, and works that may be well known only in later editions or arrangements having little relationship to the original compositions.

Earlier American Music is planned around several types of musical scores to be reprinted from early editions of the eighteenth, nineteenth, and early twentieth centuries. The categories are as follows:

- Songs and other solo vocal music
- Choral music and part-songs
- Solo keyboard music
- Chamber music
- Orchestral music and concertos
- Dance music and marches for band
- Theater music

The idea of *Earlier American Music* originated in a paper read before the Music Library Association in February, 1968, and published under the title "A Monumenta Americana?" in the Association's journal, *Notes* (September, 1968). It seems most appropriate, therefore, for the Music Library Association to sponsor this series. We hope *Earlier American Music* will stimulate further study and performance of musical Americana.

H. Wiley Hitchcock

INTRODUCTION

Supply Belcher was born in 1751 in Stoughton, Massachusetts, where he grew up to become a tavern keeper, a fiddler, and a member of the Stoughton Musical Society, one of the earliest permanent community musical groups in America. In Stoughton he would have come into contact with William Billings, perhaps the best known of the "Yankee tunesmiths"—composers of friendly, folkish music for the singing schools of the middle and late eighteenth century, and compilers of semi-religious, semi-social, "end-opening" tunebooks like *The Harmony of Maine*.

Belcher moved north in 1785 to the area we know as the state of Maine (although until 1820 it was still only one district of Massachusetts). In 1791 he established himself in Farmington, becoming one of its leading citizens and serving as justice of the peace, principal magistrate, and representative of the town in the Massachusetts Legislature. He kept up his musical activities, too. We read of "Squire Belcher's singers" in one early diary; and when in 1796 the town journal of Hallowell reported on the music at the ceremonies celebrating the successful conclusion of the first year of the Hallowell Academy, it termed Belcher the "Handel of Maine."

By then he had published his own tunebook, *The Harmony of Maine,* containing fifty-seven plain and fuguing tunes and six anthems and set-pieces. Atypically, all were of his own composition (the usual tunebook of early American psalmody included music "borrowed" from many composers . The aim of Belcher's collection was explicitly social more than religious: "The Author presumes that the propagation of Sacred Musick will answer a valuable purpose—that it will not only be a means of forming the people into Societies, but will be ornamental to civilization." It is in this light that we should perhaps view such a splendid little piece as *Jubilant* (p. 39). Although the text is ostensibly religious, one can hardly doubt that Squire Belcher's singers in the year 1794, fresh from the successful founding of the United States, imagined its message to be more a socio-political declaration than a religious one: "Let all the nations know . . . the year of Jubilee is come"!

A small but telltale technical point in terms of the changing style of American choral music in the 1790's: although in the four-voice pieces the principal air is in the tenor voice (as had long been traditional), in the three-voice pieces it is in the topmost voice (as was eventually to become the universal way).

H. W. H.

THE HARMONY OF MAINE

THE

Harmony of Maine:

BEING

An ORIGINAL COMPOSITION of PSALM and HYMN TUNES,

Of various METRES, suitable for DIVINE WORSHIP.

WITH A

Number of FUGING PIECES and ANTHEMS.

TOGETHER WITH

A CONCISE INTRODUCTION to the GROUNDS of MUSICK, and RULES for LEARNERS.

For the USE of SINGING SCHOOLS and MUSICAL SOCIETIES.

BY S. BELCHER, of FARMINGTON, COUNTY of LINCOLN, DISTRICT of MAINE.

"Awake! thou everlasting Lyre!
That once the mighty Pindar strung,
When wrapt with more than mortal fire,
The Gods of Greece he sung."

"Awake! arrest the rapid foot of time again
With liquid notes of joy, and pleasure's tow'ring strain."

O praise ye the Lord, prepare your glad voice.—*Psalm* cxlix.

PRINTED, *Typographically*, at *BOSTON*,
BY ISAIAH THOMAS AND EBENEZER T. ANDREWS.
Sold by them at FAUST'S STATUE, No. 45, Newbury Street; and by said THOMAS in WORCESTER. Sold also by the Booksellers in Town and Country.—1794.

On MUSICK.

DOWN ſteers the BASS with grave majeſtick air,
And up the TREBLE mounts with ſhrill career;
With ſofter ſounds, in mild melodious maze,
Warbling between, the TENOR gently plays:
But if th' aſpiring ALTUS join its force,
See! like the lark, it wings its tow'ring courſe;
Then rolls the rapture thro the air around,
In the full magick melody of ſound.

'Tis thine, ſweet Power, to raiſe the thought ſublime,
Quell each rude paſſion, and the heart refine;
Soft are thy ſtrains as Gabriel's gentleſt ſtring,
Calm as the breathing zephyrs of the ſpring.

PREFACE.

AS the encouragement of Arts and Sciences is beneficial to all countries, and eſpecially where the ſettlement is new, the Author preſumes that the propagation of Sacred Muſick will anſwer a valuable purpoſe—that it will not only be a means of forming the people into Societies, but will be ornamental to civilization. He therefore preſents the following WORK *to the Public—not that he expects it would ſtand the teſt of rigid criticiſm; but as his deſign is to ſubſerve the intereſt, and promote the innocent pleaſures of the community, he hopes to meet the approbation and patronage of the candid judges of Muſick.*

He has aimed at originality in his compoſition, as much as poſſible—has ſet a number of eaſy and natural Airs, for the benefit of learners, and a variety of others, for the amuſement of thoſe who have made ſome proficiency. To pleaſe every one would be ſomething new, and to pleaſe no one, would be as new. He hopes that no piece will be condemned without a fair trial.

Thoſe who have encouraged this work by ſubſcription are reſpectfully thanked. The utmoſt pains have been taken to render it correct, and the Author ſincerely wiſhes that the purchaſers may derive a ſufficient advantage, as well as amuſement from it, to make them adequate compenſation for their expences. And as the primary and genuine intention of Pſalm Singing is to praiſe the King of Heaven, he moſt earneſtly wiſhes that as often as it is attempted, it may be attended to with a becoming decency and reverence.

N. B. All Pieces ſet in Three Parts, have the Tenor on the upper Stave.

FARMINGTON, NOV. 1794.

MUSICAL TERMS.

ADAGIO.	Denotes the ſloweſt movement ; and is the proper name of the firſt mood in common time.
Allegro.	Denotes a quick movement, and is the name of the third mood in common time.
Andante.	Implies a moderate, equal and diſtinct manner of performing.
Affettuoſo.	Tender and affectionate.
Creſcendo.	This implies that the force of the voice muſt increaſe gradually till the ſtrain is ended.
Diminuendo, or dim.	Means the reverſe of the foregoing, and is ſometimes ſet in oppoſition to it ; when properly performed they make no trifling addition to the beauties of muſic.
Duetto.	Two parts only.
Dacapo.	To conclude with the firſt ſtrain.
Divoto.	In a devout manner.
Forte or for.	Full, loud, or ſtrong.
Fortiſſimo, or fortis.	Louder than forte.
Grave.	Denotes a ſlow movement, between Adagio and Largo ; it requires alſo a ſolemn manner of ſinging.
Languiſſiant.	In a languiſhing manner.
Meaſtoſo.	Paſſages which have this term placed over them muſt be performed ſlow and with majeſty and grandeur.
Moderato.	Somewhat ſlower than the true time.
Mezza piano.	Not ſo ſoft as piano.
Piano, or Pia.	Directs the performer to ſing ſoft like an echo.
Pianiſſimo or pianis.	Very ſoft.
Solo.	One part alone.
Vivace.	In a lively, cheerful manner.
Vigoroſo.	With ſtrength and firmneſs.

THE

HARMONY OF MAINE.

An INTRODUCTION to the GROUNDS of MUSICK; and RULES for LEARNERS.

Of the SCALE *of* MUSICAL NOTES, *commonly called the* GAMUT.

MUSICK is written on five lines, which, including the ſpaces between them, and immediately above and below them, are called by muſicians, a *ſtave*, and are thus placed,

It often happens that notes of muſick aſcend above, or deſcend below, theſe five lines, and then another line is occaſionally added, and is called the *Ledger Line.* Notes on the upper ledger line, are called notes in *Alt*, and thoſe on the lower ledger line, are called *Doubles.*

Theſe lines and ſpaces are repreſented by the firſt ſeven letters of the alphabet, which are placed on the ſtave, according to the part of muſick for which it is deſigned. The parts of church muſick are commonly four, viz. *Treble*, *Counter*, *Tenor*, and *Baſs.* The letters are placed on the *Treble* and *Tenor* ſtave in the following order,

Treble and *Tenor.*

G
F ———
E
D ———
C
B ———
A
G ———
F
E ———
D

Every part of muſick has, placed at the beginning of the ſtave, what is called a *Cliff*, or a muſical character which ſhews what part of the muſick is on that ſtave—whether *Treble*, *Tenor*, *Counter*, or *Baſs.*

The *Treble* and *Tenor* cliff is the ſame. It is always placed on G, the lower line but one in the *Treble* and *Tenor* ſtave, and is therefore called the *G Cliff*, and is thus marked, 

In *Counter* the letters on the ſtave are thus placed,

Counter. 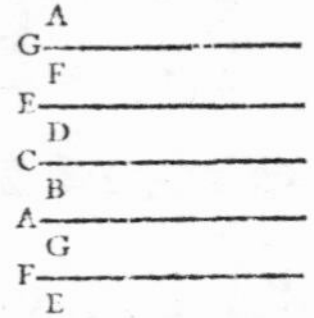
A
G
F
E
D
C
B
A
G
F
E

The *Counter* cliff, thus marked, is called the *C Cliff*, being always placed on that letter, which is the middle line of the *Counter* ſtave, and is now uſed only for this part of muſick. 

In *Baſs* the ſeven letters are thus placed on the ſtave, *viz.*

Baſs. 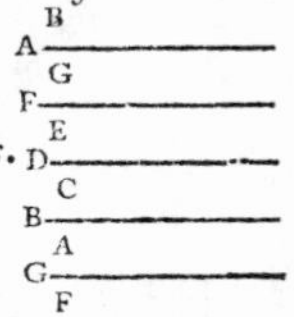
B
A
G
F
E
D
C
B
A
G
F

The third and laſt cliff is the *F Cliff*, uſed only in *Baſs*, and always placed on *F*, the upper line but one in the *Baſs* ſtave, and is thus marked, 

If either of the cliffs be moved to another line or ſpace, the letters in the order before placed, muſt all move with it; but in modern compoſitions of muſick, this ſeldom or ever happens.

Although there are more than ſeven places on the ſtave to be named by letters, yet there are but ſeven letters uſed, every eighth being the ſame repeated, and they always keep the ſame order; wherever G is found, the next letter above is A, the next B, and ſo on, always reckoning both lines and ſpaces.

All notes of muſick which repreſent ſounds, are called, in ſounding of them, by four names only, viz. *Me, fa, ſol, la.* * *Me*, is the leading note, and when that is found, the notes on the lines and ſpaces above are called *fa, ſol, la, fa, ſol, la*; and thoſe below *me, la, ſol, fa, la, ſol, fa*; after which *me* will come again; as in the following example of the *Treble*, or *Tenor*.

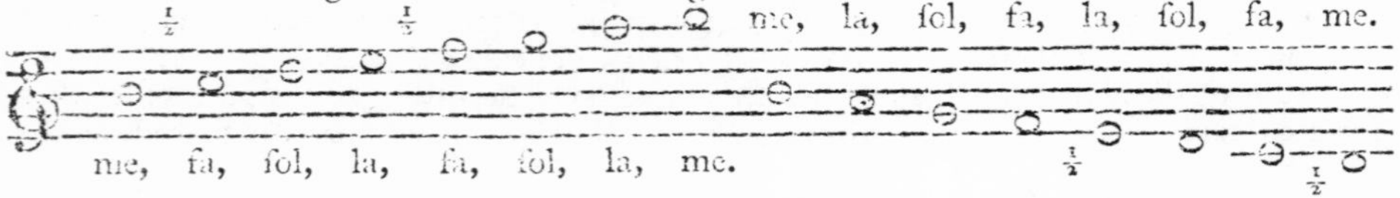
½
½
me, la, ſol, fa, la, ſol, fa, me.
me, fa, ſol, la, fa, ſol, la, me.
½
½

In *Counter* and *Baſs*, after finding *me*, the other notes are named in the ſame order.

---

* Be careful to ſpeak the notes plain. *Me* is commonly wrote *mi*, but I have called it *me* through the whole of this Introduction, as it is ſo ſounded. Sound *fa*, as in *father*; *la*, as in *lath*; and *ſol*, as in *ſoldier*.

I would here beg leave to obſerve, that the reaſon and origin of uſing figures at the beginning of the ſtave to denote the time, ſeems to be almoſt loſt, and they are called three *to* two, or three *from* two, 3 *to* 4—3 *from* 8, &c. without ſeeming any thing more than arbitrary characters, to denote a quicker or ſlower time. I think it may be of ſome uſe to explain this matter.

At firſt the *notes*, inſtead of the *names* of *ſemibreve, minim, crotchet*, &c. were called by the names of *numbers*, denoting their relative quantities or lengths. Thus a *ſemibreve* being called *one*, a *minim* was called 2, a *crotchet* 4, a *quaver* 8, *ſemiquaver* 16, &c. And $\frac{3}{2}$, means three minims in a bar, $\frac{3}{4}$, three crotchets; $\frac{3}{8}$, three quavers; $\frac{6}{4}$, ſix crotchets; $\frac{6}{8}$, ſix quavers in a bar;—and in common time, $\frac{2}{4}$, means two crotchets. And ſo of ſeveral other times which are now little uſed; as, $\frac{3}{16}$, $\frac{6}{16}$, $\frac{9}{8}$, $\frac{9}{16}$, $\frac{12}{4}$, $\frac{12}{8}$, $\frac{12}{16}$, the upper figure denoting the number of notes in a bar, and the lower figure, the name, or what kind of notes they are. (*For the various modes of time ſee page ten.*)

There are ſaid to be but *ſeven* natural ſounds, every eighth ſound being the ſame, and is called an *Octave* ; therefore theſe ſounds are repreſented by only *ſeven* letters. The ſounds are called in muſick *Tones*, five of them are called whole tones, and two of them ſemitones, or half notes. The ſemitones are between B and C, and between E and F, as marked in the foregoing example.

Although this is the natural ſituation of the ſemitones, yet their places on the ſtaves, are very often altered by flats and ſharps ; therefore obſerve, that

The *natural* place for *me*, is, in all parts of muſick, on that line or ſpace of the ſtave which is called B :

But if B be flat, ♭ *me* is in - - - - - - - - -	E	If F be ſharp ※ *me* is in - - - - - - - - -	F
B ♭ and E ♭ it is in - - - - - - - -	A	F ※ and C ※ it is in - - - - - - - -	C
B ♭ E ♭ and A ♭ it is in - - - - - -	D	F ※ C ※ and G ※ it is in - - - - - - -	G
B ♭ E ♭ A ♭ and D ♭ it is in - - - - - -	G	F ※ C ※ G ※ and D ※ it is in - - - - - -	D

As in the following example, *viz*.

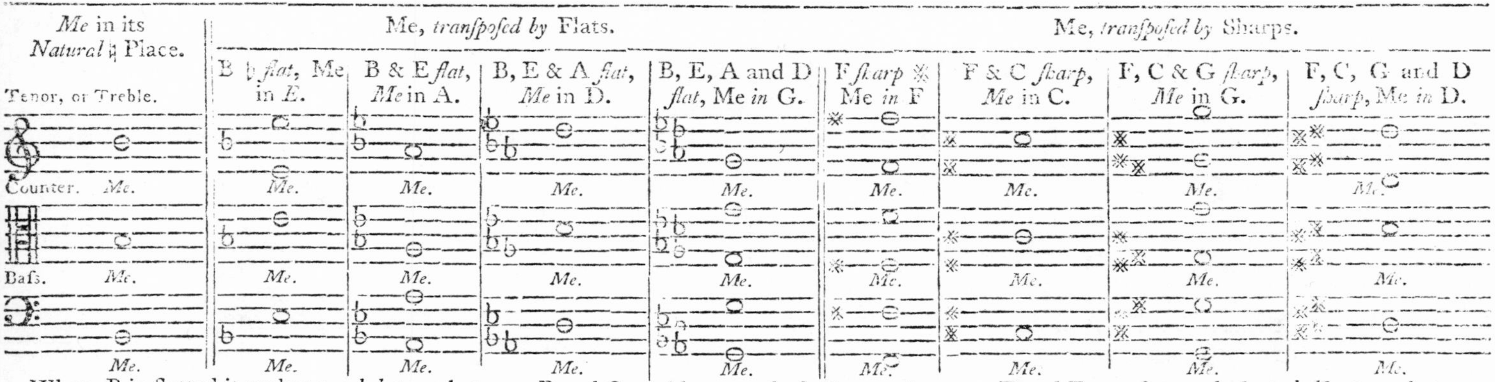

Me in its *Natural* ♮ Place.
Me, *tranſpoſed by* Flats.
Me, *tranſpoſed by* Sharps.
B ♭ *flat*, Me in *E*.
B & E *flat*, *Me* in A.
B, E & A *flat*, *Me* in D.
B, E, A and D *flat*, Me *in* G.
F *ſharp* ※ Me *in* F
F & C *ſharp*, *Me* in C.
F, C & G *ſharp*, *Me* in G.
F, C, G and D *ſharp*, Me *in* D.
Tenor, or Treble.
Counter.
Baſs.

When B is flatted it makes a *whole* tone between B and C, and leaves only *half* a tone between E and F, conſequently but *half* a tone between F and G. The reaſon of this is the alteration of *me* ; for, find *me* where you will, the notes *above*, are called as before obſerved, *fa*, *ſol*, *la*, &c. and *below*, *la*, *ſol*, *fa*, &c. and the two ſemitones are always found between *me* and *fa*, and *la* and *fa*.

A diſtinction ſhould always be made between the two ſounds of *B-me* and *C-fa* : Many are apt to ſtrike *B-me* as high as *C-fa* in ſharp keyed tunes, which injures the compoſition.

The

The NAMES *and* MEASURES *of the* NOTES *uſed in* MUSICK, *with their* RESTS.

1. *Semibreve.* 1 Bar.	2. *Minim.* ½ Bar.	3. *Crotchet.* ¼ Bar.	4. *Quaver.* ⅛ Bar.	5. *Semiquaver.* 1/16 Bar.	6. *Demiſemiquaver.* 1/32 Bar.

NOTES.
RESTS.

The following SCALE will ſhew at one View the *Proportion* one Note bears to another.

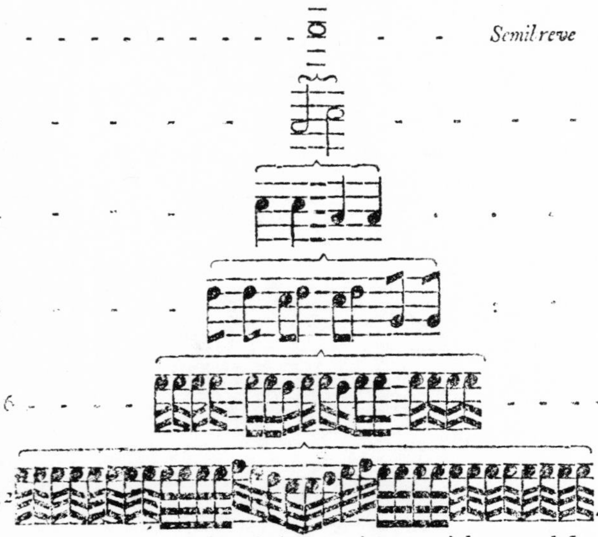

1 - - - - - - - - - - - - - - *Semibreve* - Contains

2 - - - - - - - - - - - - *Minims.*

4 - - - - - - - - *Crotchets.*

8 - - - - - - - *Quavers.*

16 - - - - - - - - *Semiquavers.*

32 *Demi-ſemiquavers.*

EXPLANATION *of the* SCALE.

THIS Scale comprehends the ſix muſical *notes*, with their reſts, and the proportion they bear to each other.

1. The *Semibreve*, is now the longeſt note uſed in muſick, though anciently it was the ſhorteſt. It is the meaſure note, and guideth all others.

2. The *Minim*, is but half the length of the ſemibreve, and has a tail to it.

3. The *Crotchet* is but half the length of the minim, and has a black head.

4. The *Quaver* is but half the length of the crotchet, having one turn to its tail, which is crooked, ſometimes one way and ſometimes another, as thus,

5. The *ſemiquaver* is half the length of the quaver, having *two* turns to its tail, which turns are crooked as variouſly as that of the quaver.

6. The *Demiſemiquaver* is half the length of the ſemiquaver, and has three turns to its tail, crooked like thoſe of the ſemiquaver.

Theſe notes are ſounded ſometimes quicker, and ſometimes ſlower, according to the ſeveral moods of time hereafter to be explained; the notes of themſelves always bear the ſame proportion to each other, whatever the time may be. All

All *Reſts*  are notes of ſilence, which ſignify that you muſt reſt, or keep ſilent, ſo long time as it takes to ſound the notes they repreſent: Excepting the *Semibreve Reſt*, which is called the *Bar Reſt*, always filling a bar, let the mood of time be what it may.

Reſts alſo help to fill bars at the beginning and end of tunes.

Beſides theſe reſts there are others, made uſe of in inſtrumental muſick, which are as follow,

2 Bars.
4 Bars.
8 Bars.

Of other CHARACTERS *uſed in* MUSICK, *and their* USES.

1.
2.
3.
4.
5.
6.
7.
8.
9.
10.
:S:
11.
tr.
12.
13.
14
Point of Addition.
Point of Diminution.
Flat.
Sharp.
Natural.
Slur.
Direct.
Bar.
Double Bar.
Repeat.
Shake, or Trill.
Double Ending.
Notes of Diſtinction.
Cloſe.

1. THE *Point of Addition*, ſet at the right hand of any note, adds to the time of that note *half* as much as it was before. When this point is ſet to a ſemibreve, it is as long as three minims, &c. as for example, 

2. A *Figure of* 3, or *Diminution*, ſet over or under any three notes, ſhews that they muſt be reduced to the time of *two* notes of the ſame kind, as for example,  which ſhews that when this figure is ſet over *three* crotchets, they muſt be ſung in the time of *one* minim, and *three* quavers, with this figure, in the time of *one* crotchet.

3. A *Flat* ♭ is a mark of *Depreſſion*, and cauſeth any note before which it is placed to be ſounded *half a tone lower* than if the flat was not there; and when a flat is ſet at the beginning of a ſtave, it has the influence of *flatting* all ſuch notes as happen to be on that line or ſpace through the whole ſtrain, unleſs regulated by the intervention of ſharps, or naturals, which anſwer only for thoſe notes where thoſe naturals or ſharps are placed, and reſpect the tone of thoſe notes only, but do not alter their names.

4. A *Sharp* ※ is a mark of *Elevation*, juſt the reverſe of the flat, and raiſes all the notes before which it is placed, *half a tone higher*: If ſet at the beginning of a ſtave, it ſharpens, or raiſes every note on that line or ſpace throughout the ſtrain, except contradicted by flats or naturals.

5. A *Natural* ♮ is a mark of *Reſtoration*, which being ſet before any note, that was made flat, or ſharp, at the beginning of a ſtave, reſtores it to its former natural tone, as for example,  Here you may ſee that B is made flat at the beginning of a ſtave, but the note which ſtands on B muſt be ſung as if there had been no flat there, becauſe it is reſtored by the *Natural* placed before it.

6. A *Slur* or *Tie*, links any number of notes together which should be sung to *one* syllable, * as for example,

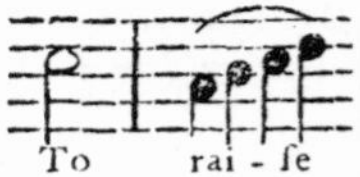
To rai - se

7. A *Direct*, is placed only at the end of lines, to direct the performer to the place of the first note, in the next line.

8. A *Bar* is used to divide the musick according to the measure note, into equal parts.

9. A *Double Bar* shews the end of a strain, and in modern musick, is commonly preceded by a *Repeat*.

10. A *Repeat* :S: shews that a *part* of the tune is to be sung *twice*, beginning the second time of singing, at the note over which it is placed, and ending a the next *Double Bar*, or *Close* : Therefore having sung that part once you must immediately sing it again.

11. A *Shake*, *tr.* or *Trill*, is or ought to be placed over any note that is, or ought to be shaken, something like the following

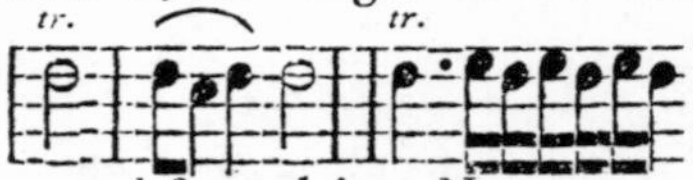
tr.
tr.

This is called one of the graces in musick ; but unless it is well done, it had better be unattempted by the performer, and sung plain. Notes may sometimes be *graced*, but not *disgraced*. Observe that a note cannot be shaken without breaking of it to pieces, as in the example : See the minim marked with a *tr.* and the example how to perform it.

12. A *Double Ending*, shewn by the figures 1 2 set over notes at the close of a tune, when there is a repeat, thus,

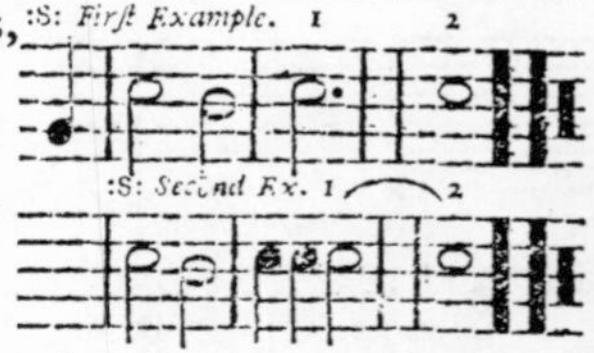
:S: First Example. 1
2
:S: Second Ex. 1
2

informs the singer, that the note under figure 1, is sung *before* the repeat, and the note under 2 must be sung the *second* time, omitting the note under figure 1. But if the notes are tied, as in the second example, then *both* notes are sung the *second* time.

13. Such notes as have *Marks of Distinction* placed over or under them, should be sounded very distinct, and with some emphasis, thus,

14. A *Close*, is two, three, or four bars together, which shew the tune to be ended.

* In singing slurred notes in words, great care should be taken to pronounce the words properly, for which purpose observe these directions : Keep your lips and teeth asunder from the beginning to the end of the slur, warble tne notes in your throat, sliding easily from one sound to another, without any kind of hitch or jolt, (which is too often practised) and if possible do not stop to take breath until you you have done ; otherwise you break the slur and spoil the pronunciation.

Of the various MOODS *of* TIME *used in* PSALMODY.

NINE different Moods of Time are now used in Psalmody, *four* of which are called *Common Time*, viz. *Adagio*, *Largo*, *Allegro*, and 2, 4, or 2 *Fours*, and are thus characterized at the beginning of tunes or strains, *viz.*

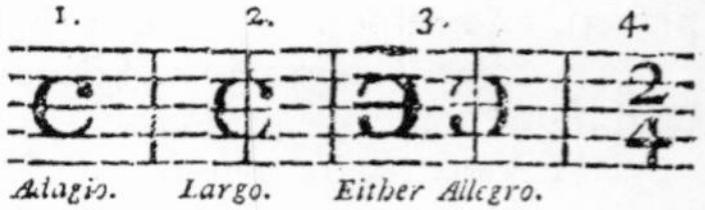
1.
2.
3.
4.
Adagio.
Largo.
Either Allegro.

These four are called common time, because they are measured by even numbers, as 2, 4, 8, &c. *Adagio*, denotes a very slow movement : It has a semibreve for its measure note ; every bar containing that or other notes or rests amounting to the same quantity of time ; so in the example following, a semibreve fills the *first* bar ; the *second* bar is filled by *four* crotchets ; the *third* bar by a semibreve rest. In order to give these notes and rests their proper regular time,

time, a motion of the hand is neceſſary, which is calling *Beating of Time* ; every motion or ſwing of the hand, is called a *Beat*. This mood has *four* beats in a bar, which ſhould be beaten two down, and *two* up, in the following manner,

Adagio. 1, 2, 3, 4.
1, 2, 3, 4.
1, 2, 3, 4.
d, d, u, u.
d, d, u, u.
d, d, u, u.

Firſt, lightly ſtrike the ends of your fingers : *Secondly*, the heel of your hand : *Thirdly*, raiſe your hand a little, and ſhut it partly up : *Fourthly*, raiſe it ſtill higher, and throw it open at the ſame time ; which completes the bar. It is beſt to diſtinguiſh the third motion from the fourth, by ſhutting or opening the hand. Every bar in this mood of time is performed in the like manner. Each beat ſhould be exactly one ſecond of time.

Largo, the *ſecond* mood in common time, has likewiſe a *ſemibreve* for its meaſure note, and contains notes or reſts to that amount, in each bar This alſo has *four* beats to a bar, performed in the ſame manner as in Adagio, only one quarter quicker, or *four beats* in the time of *three ſeconds*.

Largo. 1, 2, 3, 4.
1, 2, 3, 4.
1, 2, 3, 4.
d. d. u. u.
d. d. u. u.
d. d. u. u.

Where the muſic, in *Largo*, conſiſts chiefly of minims, ſometimes but *two* beats are given to a bar.

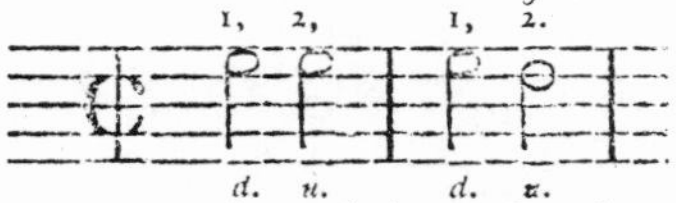
1, 2,
1, 2.
d. u.
d. u.

Allegro, the *third* common time mood, has alſo a *ſemibreve* for its meaſure note, and contains notes or reſts to that amount, in each bar ; but has only two beats to a bar, which are *one* down, and *one* up, allowing one ſecond to each beat, as in the example.

Allegro. 1, 2.
1, 2.
1, 2.
d. u.
d. u.
d. u.

The *fourth* common time mood, 2, 4, or 2 *fours*, has a *minim* for its meaſure note, and notes or reſts to that amount in each bar ; it has alſo *two* beats to a bar, *one* down, and *one* up. *Four* beats in this time, are performed as quick as *three* in *Largo*, when four beats are given to *that* mood of time. *(See note at the bottom of page 6th.)*

1, 2.
1, 2.
1, 2.
d.u.
d. u.
d. u.

The next moods of time in order, are called *Triple Time* moods, of which there are *three*, viz. 3 *Twos* ; 3 *Fours* ; and 3 *Eights*. They are called *Triple*, becauſe they are meaſured by odd numbers, each bar containing either *three* minims, *three* crotchets, or *three* quavers ; *two* of which muſt be ſung with the hand down, and *one* up. The marks of triple time are thus ſet at the beginning of ſtaves,

The *firſt*, 3 *Twos*, contains *three* minims, or *one* pointed ſemibreve, or other notes which meaſure equal to them, in a bar ; which are ſung in the time of three ſeconds, *two* beats down, and *one* up, as in the example.

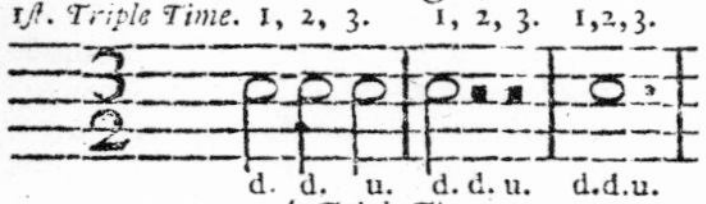
1ſt. Triple Time. 1, 2, 3.
1, 2, 3.
1,2,3.
d. d. u.
d. d. u.
d.d.u.

N. B. A minim in 3 *Twos* is performed in the ſame time as a crotchet in the firſt mood of common time.

The *ſecond* mood of triple time, 3 *fours*; contains *three* crotchets, or other notes or reſts equivalent, in a bar, which has *three* beats, *two* down, and the other up, one half quicker than the firſt triple time mood : A crotchet in this time is equal to a crotchet in the ſecond mood of common time.

Example.

2d. Triple-Time. 1, 2, 3.
1, 2, 3.
1, 2, 3.
d, d, u.
d, d, u.
d, d, u.

The *third* triple time mood, has *three* quavers, or one pointed crotchet, or other notes, or reſts, equivalent, in a bar ; has alſo *three* beats to a bar, but they are performed as quick again as in the mood laſt mentioned.

3d. Triple Time. 1, 2, 3.
1,2, 3.
1, 2, 3.
d, d, u.
d,d, u.
d. d.u.

The

The two remaining moods are called *Compound Moods* ; being compounded of common and triple meaſure ; of common, as the bar is divided equally, the fall being equal to the riſe ; and of triple, as each half of the bar is threefold.

The two compound moods are diſtinguiſhed, at the beginning of ſtaves, thus,

The *firſt*, 6 *Fours*, contains *ſix crotchets* in a bar, or other notes or reſts equivalent, which are ſung in the time of *two* ſeconds, and by *two* equal beats, one down and one up, as in the example following :

1ſt. Comp. Mood.
1, 2.
1, 2.
d.
u.
d.
u.

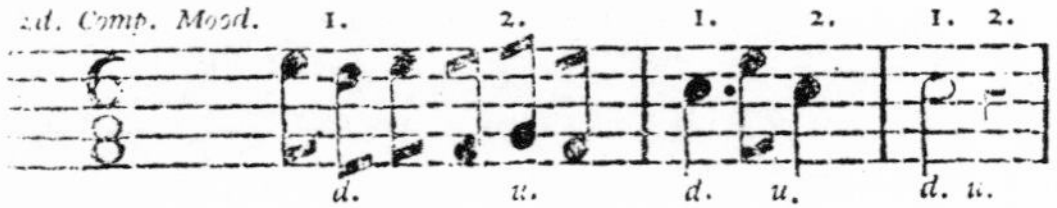
2d. Comp. Mood.
1.
2.
1.
2.
1.
2.
d.
u.
d.
u.
d.
u.

The *ſecond* compound mood, contains *ſix quavers* in a bar ; has alſo *two* beats to a bar, one down and one up. A beat in this mood has the ſame time as the ſecond in common time, called *Largo*.*

Of

* The figures in the examples placed over the bars ſhew the number of beats in each bar, and the letters placed under the bars ſhew how they muſt be beat, viz. the letter *d* ſhews when the hand muſt go *down*, and the letter *u*, when it muſt riſe *up*.

The bar reſt is properly ſo called, becauſe it is allowed to fill a bar in all moods of time.

Obſerve here——That the hand falls at the beginning, and riſes at the end of every bar, in all moods of time.

That in the Adagio and Largo moods, a ſemibreve is four beats, a minim two, a crotchet one, a quaver half, &c.

That in the Allegro and 3, 2, moods, a ſemibreve is two beats, a minim one, a crotchet half, &c.

That in the 2, 4 ; 3, 4 ; 3, 8, and 6, 8, moods, a ſemibreve cannot be uſed, becauſe that it will more than fill a bar.

That in 3, 8, where a minim cannot be uſed, a crotchet is two beats, a quaver one, &c.

That in 6, 4, a pointed minim is one beat, crotchets three at a beat, &c.

That in 6, 8, a pointed crotchet is one beat, quavers three at a beat, &c.

Obſerve alſo—— That in thoſe moods of time which are not marked with figures, a ſemibreve fills a bar ; but in all thoſe moods which are marked with figures, the upper figure expreſſes a certain number of notes of ſome kind which fill a bar, and the under figure ſhews how many of that kind of notes are equal to a ſemibreve ; ſo in the mood marked 3, 2, the upper figure being 3, ſhews that three notes of ſome kind will fill a bar in that mood, and the under figure 2, ſhews that two of them are equal to a ſemibreve ; now two minims are equal to a ſemibreve, therefore three minims fill a bar in that mood of time. The ſame rule holds good with regard to the other moods marked with figures.

The performing the ſeveral moods in their proper time, is a matter which ſhould be well attended to : And yet ſingers often fail in this point. That ſome moods are quicker and ſome ſlower, all agree, yet ſome will ſing every mood alike, or ſo nearly alike that the difference is ſcarcely perceptible. This, in many pieces, eſpecially in ſuch as change from one mood to another, entirely fruſtrates the deſign of the compoſer, and ruins the muſick. Others again will ſing all moods too ſlow : This is ſo common that many perſons who profeſs to be good ſingers will ſcarcely allow it to be an error. It is generally moſt prevalent in thoſe companies where the ſpirit of muſick is upon the decline, and the ſingers grown dull and indifferent about ſinging ; they will then drag on heavily through a piece of muſick, and render it not only a burden to themſelves, but diſagreeable to all who hear them. On the other hand, ſome may err by beating time too faſt ; this error is ſometimes found in perſons who are poſſeſſed of too great a ſhare

of

Tenor.

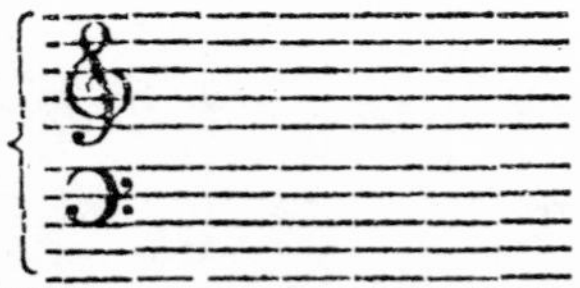

Baſs.

Of the BRACE.

THE ſeveral parts of a piece of muſick, which are ſung together, are ſhewn by a *Brace*, placed at the beginning of the ſtaves, as in the example. If *two* parts only are ſung together, the brace, or *two* perpendicular lines, encloſe the two ſtaves ; and if three parts are ſung together, then the brace is extended to encloſe *three*, and ſo of *four*.

Of CHUSING NOTES.

NOTES are often ſet immediately over each other in the ſame ſtave and bar, only *one* of which is to be ſounded by the ſame perſon ; the ſinger may ſound which of them he pleaſes : If two perſons are ſinging the ſame part, one of them may take the *upper* note, and the other the *lower* note.

Example of chuſing Notes.

Notes ſet an *eighth* below the *common Baſs*, are called *Ground Baſs*. Reſts are often placed over each other, but the time of *both* is to be reckoned.

Of the ſeveral CONCORDS *and* DISCORDS, *both perfect and imperfect.* [From *Tanſur's* Royal Mel.]

THERE are but four *Concords* in muſick, viz. *Uniſon, Third, Fifth,* and *Sixth* ; (their *Eighths* or *Octaves* are alſo meant.) The *Uniſon* is called a *perfect cord* ; and commonly the *Fifth* is ſo called ; but the *Fifth* may be made *imperfect*, if the compoſer pleaſes.—The *Third* and *Sixth*, are called *imperfect* ; their *cords* not being ſo full, nor ſo ſweet as the *perfect* : But in four parts, the *Sixth* is often uſed inſtead of the *Fifth*, in ſome certain places, when the *Fifth* is left out ; ſo in effect, there are but three *concords*, employed together, in *compoſition*.

N. B. The meaning of the word *Imperfect*, ſignifies, that it wants a *ſemitone* of its *perfection*, to what it does when it is perfect ; for, as the *leſſer*, or *imperfect Third*, includes but three *half tones* ; the *greater* or *major Third*, includes four *half tones*, &c. The

of oſtentation. To enable young ſingers and young teachers of muſick to avoid all theſe errors, and to give each mood its proper time, I have added the following directions. Take a leaden ball, the ſize whereof is immaterial ; about an inch in diameter is as well as any : Suſpend it by a ſmall tight cord in ſuch a manner as that it may ſwing each way without interruption, and for the ſeveral moods of time, let the length of the cord from the centre of the ball to the pin or nail from which it is ſuſpended be as follows :

For the Adagio, Allegro, 3, 2 and 6, 4 moods, $39\frac{2}{10}$ Inches.
For the Largo, 3, 4 and 6, 8 moods, ——— $22\frac{1}{20}$ ———
For 2, 4 ——— ——— ——— ——— $12\frac{4}{10}$ ———
For 3, 8 ——— ——— ——— ——— $5\frac{1}{21}$ ———

Then for every ſwing or vibration of the ball, i. e. every time that it croſſes the perpendicular line, or place of its natural ſituation when at reſt, count one beat, and for the different moods of time according to the different lengths of the cord as expreſſed above. This is ſo eaſy a way of aſcertaining the true time for each mood, that it is preſumed no one who deſigns to be a ſinger will think it too much trouble to make trial of it.

Theſe moods are however, ſometimes varied from their true time, by arbitrary words, ſuch as quick, ſlow, &c. being placed over the tune or anthem, in which caſe no certain rules can be given : The following general directions however may not be amiſs.

When the term ſlow occurs, let the muſick be performed about one ſixth ſlower than the true time, and when the term very ſlow occurs, about as much ſlower ſtill, and contrary for terms quick and very quick.

The *Diſcords*, are a *Second*, a *Fourth*, and a *Seventh*, and their *Octaves*; though ſometimes the *greater Fourth* comes very near to the *ſound* of an *imperfect cord*, it being the ſame in *ratio* as the *minor Fifth*. But I will ſet you

An Example *of the ſeveral* CONCORDS *and* DISCORDS, *with their* OCTAVES *under them*.

	CONCORDS.				DISCORDS.		
Single Cords—	1.	3.	5.	6.	2.	4.	7.
Their *Octaves, or Eighths*—	8	10	12	13	9	11	14
	15	17	19	20	16	18	21
	22	24	26	27	23	25	28 &c.

N. B. That if a *voice*, or *inſtrument*, could reach to ten thouſand *Octaves*, they are all counted as one, in nature.

Every *Eighth*, or *Octave*, contains *twelve* ſemitones, the *five whole* tones being divided into *ſemitones*, and the two *natural* ſemitones, make the twelve. As in the following example.

An OCTAVE contains 12 Semitones.

G		8th	12
f♯ or g♭	♯	7th	11
F	♭	7th	10
E	♯	6th	9
e♭ or d♯	♭	6th	8
D		5th	7
c♯ or d♭	♯	4th	6
C		4th	5
B	♯	3d	4
b♭ or a♯	♭	3d	3
A	♯	2d	2
g♯ or a♭	♭	2d	1
G		uniſon.	0

In this ſcale of *Semitones*, the lower line G is made the foundation from which the others are reckoned, and is therefore called a *Uniſon*, becauſe one and the ſame ſound is a uniſon. The right hand column of figures ſhews the number of ſemitones between G at the bottom and each of the other letters, both in their natural ſituation, and when made flat or ſharp. Next above G you will find G ſharp, or A flat, which is called a flat ſecond, containing but one ſemitone; the next is A, which is a ſharp ſecond, containing two ſemitones; the next is B flat, or A ſharp, which is a flat third, containing three ſemitones; the next is B, which is a ſharp third, containing four ſemitones; the next is C, which is a fourth, containing five ſemitones, &c. &c. The flat ſecond, third, ſixth and ſeventh, are called leſſer ſeconds, thirds, &c. and the ſharp ſecond, third, fourth, ſixth and ſeventh, are called greater ſeconds, thirds, &c. which is the common diſtinction, and the greater always contains a ſemitone more than the leſſer.

Of the KEYS *uſed in Muſick.*

IN Muſick there are only two *natural*, or primitive Keys; one of which is cheerful, and called *ſharp*; the other melancholy, and called *flat*. C is called the ſharp key, and A the flat key. Without the aid of flats and ſharps placed at the beginning of ſtaves, no tune can rightly be formed on any other than *natural* keys. Flats and ſharps placed at the beginning of ſtaves tranſpoſe B-me, the centre and maſter note, together with all the reſt in their order, and by forming what are called *artificial keys*, bring the ſame effect as the two natural keys. The reaſon why the two natural keys are tranſpoſed by flats and ſharps at the beginning of the ſtaves, is, to bring them within the compaſs of the voice. The laſt note in the Baſs is the *key note*, and is immediately *above*, or *below me*; if above, it is a ſharp key; and if below, it is a flat key; or in plainer terms—all tunes are either on a *ſharp* or a *flat* key; if the laſt note of the Baſs, or *key note* is named *fa*, then it is a ſharp key; but if it is named *la* then it is a flat key. The *key* note can never properly be *me*, or *ſol*. The reaſon why one tune is on a ſharp, lively key, and another on a flat, melancholy one, is that every third, ſixth and ſeventh, in the ſharp key, is half a tone higher than in the flat key. See the following example of the two keys.

A

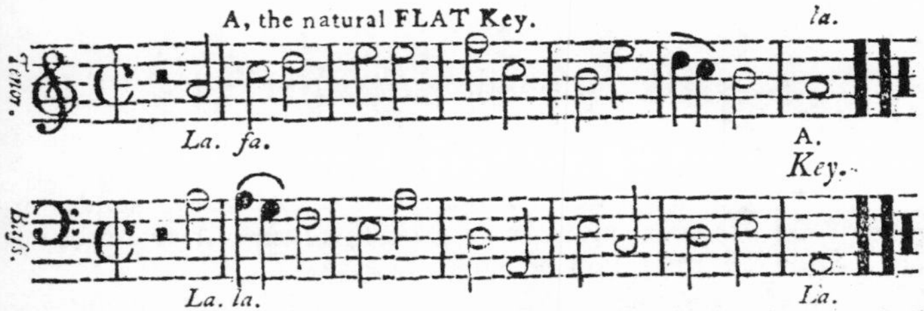
A, the natural FLAT Key.
la.
Tenor.
La. fa.
A.
Key.
Bass.
La. la.
La.

C, the natural SHARP Key.
fa.
Tenor.
Fa. la.
C.
Key.
Bass.
Fa. fa.
Fa.

Of LEADING NOTES.

THE Appogiatura, or leading note, ferves for the arriving more gracefully to the following note, either rifing or falling, and muft be dwelt on according to the length of the note it is made of; fometimes it is ufed as a preparation to a trill, and is expreffed by an intermediate note, or notes: As for example.

N. B. Obferve the *little notes* are not reckoned in time, and are only to be foftly touched, or founded.

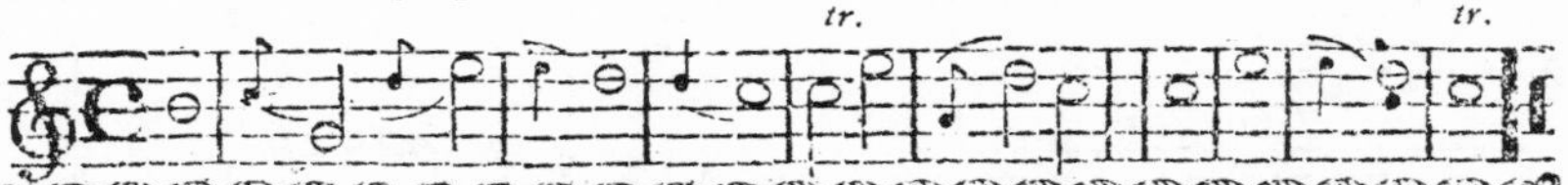
tr.
tr.

Of TRANSITION.

THE *little notes* flurred to the minims muft not be confidered as adding any thing to the time, the bars being full without them, but only as notes to lead the voice from one found to another, and if founded at all, muft be founded as much fofter than the minims as they are fmaller. Tranfition is nothing but fliding gracefully from one note to another: But fingers fhould be exceedingly careful to deviate as little as poffible from the true found of a note, becaufe in going off from the true found they will undoubtedly make difcords where the compofer did not defign to have any, and then perhaps the compofition will be defpifed, becaufe the performers are faulty.

" N. B. Tranfition, as well as trills, had better be omitted than badly performed."

Of SYNCOPATION.

NOTES of Syncopation are thofe which are driven out of their proper order in the bar, or driven through it, and require the hand to be taken up or put down, while fuch notes are founding. One or two examples follow, which, with the help of the mafter, will foon be underftood by the young fingers of tolerable capacities.

Examples

Examples of *Syncopation.*

The Learner may ſing the Notes as they ſtand in the following Stave.

Of the ſounding *the* EIGHT NOTES.

THOSE learners of pſalmody, who make themſelves ſufficiently acquainted with the knowledge of the Gamut, and firſt principles of vocal muſic, may proceed to tune their voices by the following notes.

Great care muſt be taken to give every note its true and diſtinct ſound, and to obſerve the ſemitones between *me* and *fa*, and *la* and *fa* in aſcending; and alſo between *fa* and *la*, and *fa* and *me*, deſcending. After having learned to ſound the following notes well, they may begin to practiſe on plain and eaſy muſick.

CONCLUSION.

THIS part of the work will be concluded with ſome obſervations on ſinging, and general directions to learners, which are as follows, *viz.*

"When a tune is well learnt by note it may be ſung in words, and every word ſhould not only be pronounced according to the beſt rules of grammar, but ſpoken plain and diſtinct. Singers often fail in this point, by which means half the beauty of the muſick is loſt, the words not being underſtood.

"Notwithſtanding all that has been ſaid or can be ſaid with regard to graces, the beſt way is to ſing with eaſe and freedom, and without confining yourſelf to any certain rules for gracing muſick, any further than can be adapted in a natural and eaſy manner, there being nothing forced or unnatural in good muſick.—Every ſinger ſhould ſing that part which is moſt ſuitable to his voice, in which caſe learners ſhould ſubmit to the judgment of their maſter. Care ſhould be taken, in ſinging companies, to have the parts properly proportioned; one half the ſtrength of the voices ſhould be upon the baſs, the other half divided upon the other parts.—A ſolo ſhould generally be ſung ſofter, and a chorus which follows a ſolo, louder than the reſt of the muſick. When the words ſoft, loud, &c. are placed over the muſick, ſome regard ſhould be paid to them. When words are repeated in muſick, the ſtrength of the voices ſhould increaſe every time they are repeated, and when the muſick is repeated it may be well to ſing it louder the ſecond time than the firſt. Low notes in the baſs ſhould generally be ſounded full, and the high notes in any part, not full, but clear. In fuging muſick the ſtrength of the voices ſhould increaſe as the parts fall in, and the pronunciation in ſuch caſes ſhould be very diſtinct and emphatical."

THE

THE

HARMONY OF MAINE.

Alpha. C. M.

Major,
My ſoul, repeat his praiſe, Whoſe mercies are ſo great; Whoſe anger is ſo ſlow to riſe, So ready to abate.
C

Majesty. C. M.

Prepare, &c.
Behold the glories of the Lamb, Amidst his father's throne! Pre -
Prepare, &c.
Prepare new honours for his
1 :S: 2
Prepare new honours for his name, And fon - - gs, before unknown.
pare new honours for his na - - - - - me, And fongs before unknown.
name, Prepare new honours for his name, And fon - - - gs before unknown.
name, Prepare new h onours for his name, And fongs before unknown.

Harmony. C. M. :S:

Ten
Come let us join our chearful fongs, With angels round the throne.
Ten thoufand thoufand
Ten thoufand thoufand are their tongues But
Ten thoufand thoufand are their tongues, But all their joys
1 :S: 2
Thoufand thoufand are their tongues, But all their joys are one. Ten, &c.
are their tongues, But all their joys are one. But all their joys, all their joys are one.
all their joys are one. Ten thoufand, &c.
o - - - - ne. Ten thoufand, &c.

Creation. L. M.

The ſpacious firmament on high, With all the blue ethereal ſky, And ſpangl'd heavens a ſhining frame, Their great o - ri - gi - nal proclaim.

Hallowell. S. M. :S:

Thy, &c.
O let thy God and King, Thy ſweeteſt tho'ts employ ; Thy children ſhall his honours ſing, In palaces of
Thy children ſhall, &c.
jo - -

Hallowell. Continued.

1 :S: 2
Thy, &c,
joy, In palaces of joy.
jo - - - - - - y. Thy children ſhall his honours ſing In palaces of joy.
1 :S: 2
- y, Thy children ſhall, &c.
jo - - - - y, In, &c.

Advent. C. M.

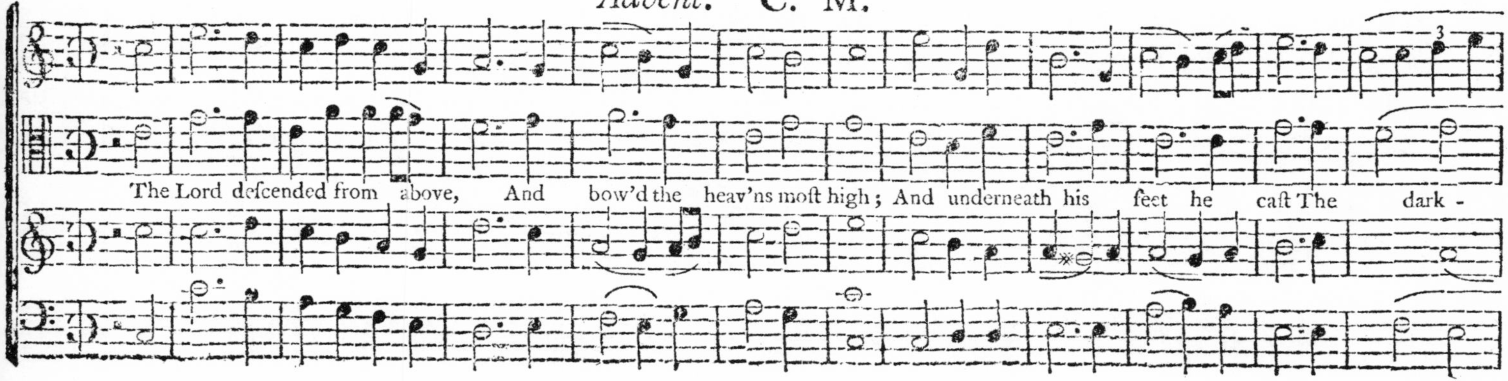
The Lord deſcended from above, And bow'd the heav'ns moſt high; And underneath his feet he caſt The dark -

On Cherubs and on Cherubims full royally he rode.
-rk - neſs of the ſky. On Cherubs and on Cherubims, full royally he rode. And on the wings of
mighty wind came fly - ing, fly - ing fly - - ing all abroad.

St. David's New. P. M.

:S:

I'll praiſe my Maker with my breath, And when my voice is loſt in death; Praiſe ſhall employ my nobler pow'rs;
My
My days of praiſe ſhall
My days of praiſe ſhall ne'er be
1
2
My days of praiſe ſhall ne'er be paſt, While life and tho't and being laſt, Or, &c.
days of praiſe ſhall ne'er be paſt, While life and tho't and be - ing laſt, Or immor - tal - i - ty endure.
ne'er be paſt, My days of praiſe ſhall ne'er be paſt, While life and tho't and being laſt, Or, &c.
paſt, While life and tho't and being laſt,

St. Paul's. S. M.

How beaut'ous, &c.
How beaut'ous are their feet, Who ſtand on Zion's hill; Who bring ſal - vation on their tongues, And
:S:
How charming is their voice, How ſweet their tidings are, Zion be-
words of peace reveal.

St. Paul's. Continued.

Fortissimo.

Zion behold thy Saviour king, he reigns, he reigns, &c.
hold thy Saviour king, He reigns and triumphs here.
thy Saviour king, he reigns he reigns,
king, thy Saviour king, He reigns, &c.

The Dawn. L. M.

Au - ro - ra veils her rosy face, When brighter Phebus takes her place, So glad will grace re-

Moderato.
ſign her room To glory in the heav'nly home.
So glad will grace reſign her room,
So glad, &c.
To glory, to glo - - - ry
To glory, to glory, glory, glory, in the heav'nly home.
To glory, to glo - - - - ry,
To glory. to glory, to glory, glory, glory,

Appearance. L. M.

Crefcendo.
The voice of my be - loved founds, Over the rocks and rifing grounds ; O'er hills of guilt and
feas of grief, He leaps, he flies to my relief. Now thro' the veil of flefh I fee, With eyes of love he looks at me, With

Now in the gospel's clearest glass, He shows the beauties
eyes of love he looks at me. Now in the gospel's clearest glass, He shows the beauties of his fa - -
Now in the gospel's clearest glass, He shows the beauties of his face, the beauties, the
Now, &c. the beauties, the beauties,
of his face, the beauties, the beau - - ties, the beau - - - ties of his face.
ce, the beauties of his face.
beau - ties, the beau - - - - ties, the beau - - - - ties of his face.
the beauties the beauties,

Transition. C. M.

Touch'd by the sun the lustre fades and weeps itself away And
When snows descend and robe the fields, In winters bright array,
Touch'd by the sun the lustre fades And
Touch'd by the sun the lustre fades And
Touch'd by the sun the lustre fades, touch'd by the sun the lustre
Diminuendo.
and weeps itself a - way and weeps, and weeps, &c.
weeps itself away, and weeps itself a way, and weeps itself away, and weeps itself a - way.
weeps itself away and weeps weeps, weeps &c.
fades And weeps itself away And weeps, weeps, weeps, &c.

Invitation. L. M.

Vivace.

Child of the ſummer, charming roſe, No longer in confinement lie ; Ariſe ! to light thy form diſcloſe,
Rival the ſpangles of the ſky, rival the ſpangles, the ſpangles of the ſky.
The rains are gone, the ſtorms are o'er,
Rival the ſpangles of the ſky, rival the ſpangles of the ſky.
Rival, &c.

Winter retires to make the way, Come then thou ſweetly bluſhing flow'r, Come lovely ſtranger come away. The ſun is dreſt in
Piano.
beaming ſmiles, To give thy beauties to the day, Young zephyrs wait with gent - leſt gales, To fan thy boſom,

Invitation. Continued.

Pianiſſimo.
fan thy boſom, to fan thy boſom as they play, to fan thy boſom as they play.

Cheſter. L. M.

How ſhall the young ſecure their hearts, And guard their lives from ſin ? Thy word the choiceſt rule imparts, To keep the conſcience clean.

The Requeſt. L. M.

Creſcendo.
Deminuendo,
Give me, O Lord, a ſoul ſo high, Whoſe vaſt dimenſions reach the ſky; That comprehends within its thought, The whole con-
Affetuoſo.
tents of good and naught. And let it be as good as great, Its higheſt throne a mercy ſeat; Diſſolving like a ſhow'r on earth, To give ten thouſand
6
4

E

Andante.
Mæſtoſo.
ſeeds a birth, Which hangs on flow'rs, and tender plants, Sucks not their ſweets, but feeds their wants. So let my talent in full flood,
pour forth in ſtreams for others good; And at the laſt, O Lord reſtore, My ſoul to joy for - ever - more.
1
2

Heroiſm. L. M.

Affetuoſo.
Why ſhould vain mortals, Tremble at the ſight of Death and deſtruction, In the field of battle,
Where blood and
Where blood and carnage,
Where blood and carnage, Clothe the ground in crimſon, Sounding,
Where blood and carnage, Clothe the ground in crimſon, Sounding, ſounding, Sounding with death groans.
carnage, Clothe the ground in crimſon, Sounding, ſounding, ſounding,
Clothe the ground in crimſon, Sounding, ſounding, ſounding, ſounding,

The Lilly. P. M.

Peaceful and lowly in their native foil, They neither know to fpin, nor care to toil ;
Yet with confefs'd mag-ni-fi-cence de - ride. Our mean attire, and impotence of pride.

Fiftieth Psalm Tune. P. M.

Grave.
The God of glory sends his summons forth, Calls the south nations, and awakes the north ; From east to west the sov'reign orders spread, Thro' distant
worlds and regions of the dead. The trumpet sounds, hell trembles, heav'n rejoices ; Lift up your heads, ye saints, with cheerful voices.

Carol. C. M.

While shepherds watch'd their flocks by night, All seated on the ground; The angel of the Lord came down, And glo - - - ry shone a-
And glo - ry, glo ry, glo - ry,
round. And glo - ry, glo - ry, glo - ry, glory shone around.
And glo - ry, glo - ry, glo - - - ry,

Jubilant. P. M.

Vigoroso.
Blow ye the trumpet blow, blow ye the trumpet blow,
Blow, &c.
Blow, &c.
The gladly solemn found, Let all the nations know, To earth's remoteft
Blow ye the trumpet blow,
Blow, &c.
Blow, &c.
Blow, &c.
Fortiſſimo.
The year of Jubilee is come, Return, &c.
bound,
The year, &c.
Return, return ye randſom'd ſinners home.
The year, &c.
Return, return,
The year of Jubilee is come, Return, return, return,

Lincoln. C. M.

Let all the juſt to God, with joy, Their cheerful voices raiſe ; For well the righteous it becomes To
Piano.
Let harps, &c.
ſing glad ſongs of praiſe. Let harps, and pſalteries, and lutes, In joyful concert
Let harps, &c. In joyful, joyful concert
Let harps, and pſalteries, and lutes, In joyful concert meet. In joyful concert

Lincoln. Continued.

Forte.
meet : And new made fongs of loud ap - - - - - plaufe, The har - mo - ny complete.
meet :

Converfion.

1 2
My rapture feem'd a pleafing dream, My rapture feem'd a pleafing dream, The grace appear'd fo great, the grace appear'd fo great.
When God reveal'd his gracious name, And chang'd my mournful ftate,
My, &c.
My, &c.
my, &c,
My raprure feem'd a pleafing dream, &c.

F

Content.

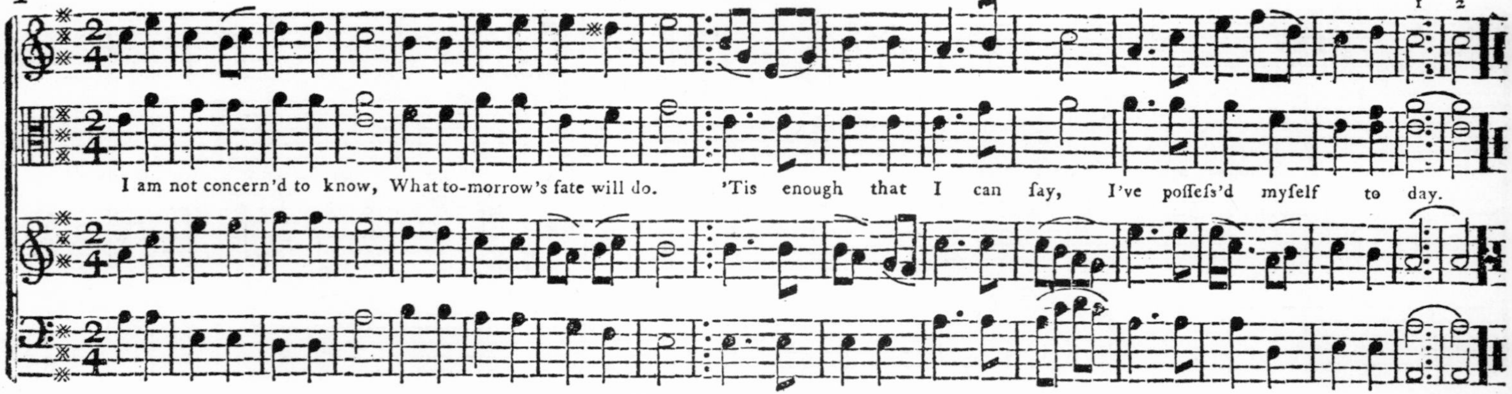
I am not concern'd to know, What to-morrow's fate will do.
'Tis enough that I can ſay, I've poſſeſs'd myſelf to day.

Reflection.

Lord, what a thoughtleſs wretch was I, To mourn, and murmur, and repine, To ſee the wicked plac'd on

Grave.
high, In pride, and robes of honor ſhine! But O their end, Their dreadful end! Thy ſanc-tu-a-ry taught me ſo:
On ſlipp'ry rocks I ſee them ſtand, And fi' - - ry billows roll be - low.

Protection.

Though earth were from her centre tost, And
God is our refuge in distress, A present help when dangers press, In him undaunted we'll confide.
Though earth were from her
Though earth, &c.
Though earth, &c.
mountains in the ocean lost, Torn peacemeal by the roaring tide,
centre tost, And mountains in the ocean lost, Torn peacemeal by the roaring tide, Torn peacemeal by the roaring tide.
1
2

Admiration. L. M.

Ye sons of men with joy record, The various wonders of the Lord, And let his pow'r and goodness
found, Thro' all your tribes the world around.
Let the high heav'ns, &c.
Let the high heav'ns, &c.
Where
Let the high heav'ns, &c.
Let the high heav'ns your songs invite, Those spacious fields of brilliant light,

ſun and moon and planets roll, And ſtars that glow from pole to
pole, Where ſun and moon, &c.

Friendſhip.

How pleaſant 'tis to ſee, Kindred and friends agree, Each in their proper ſtation move, And each ful-
fil their part, With ſympathizing heart, In all the cares of life and love.

Rapture.

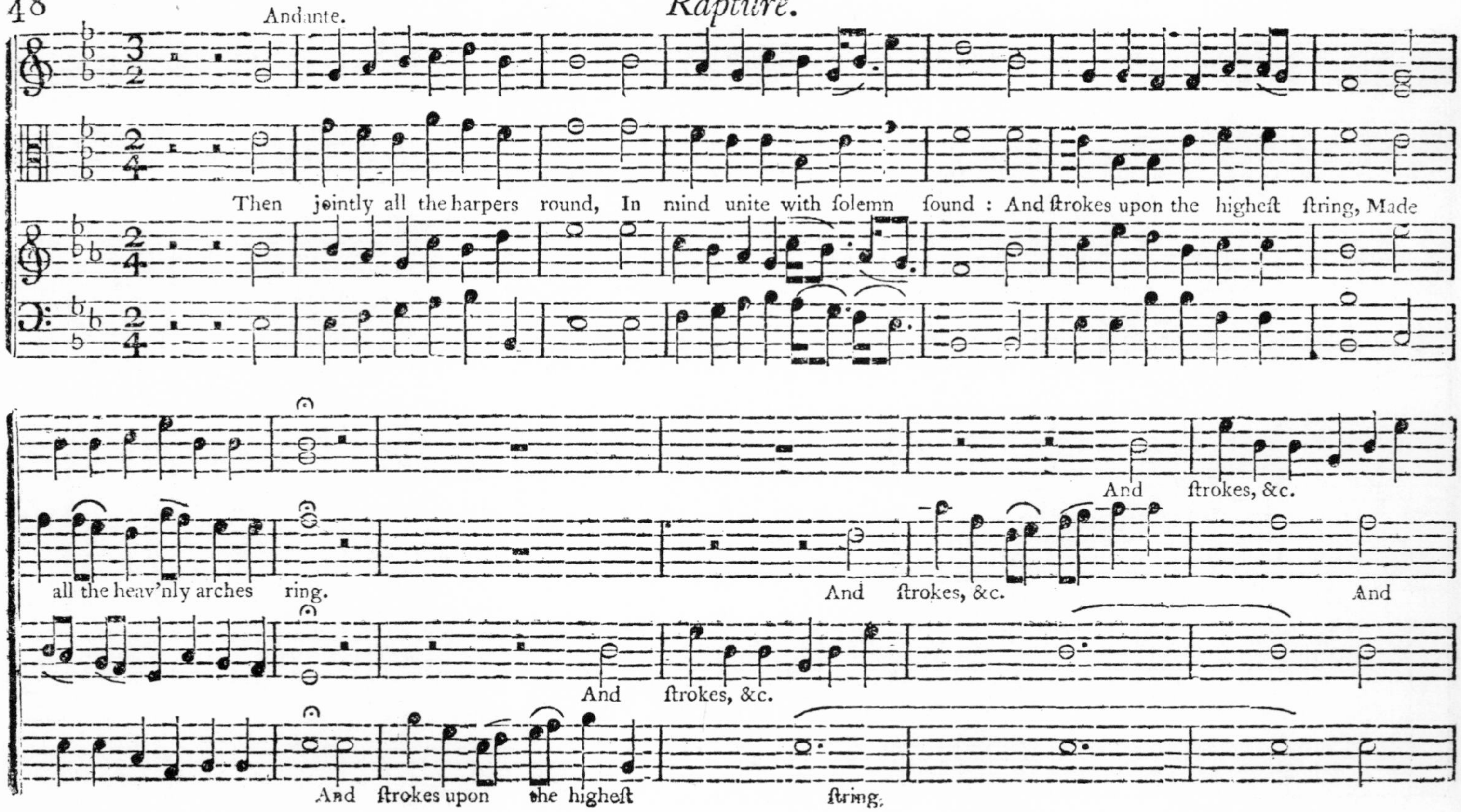
Andante.
Then jointly all the harpers round, In mind unite with ſolemn ſound : And ſtrokes upon the higheſt ſtring, Made
And ſtrokes, &c.
all the heav'nly arches ring.
And ſtrokes, &c.
And
And ſtrokes, &c.
And ſtrokes upon the higheſt ſtring.

Rapture. Continued.

Forte.
And ſtrokes, &c.
ſtrokes upon the higheſt ſtring, Made all, &c.

Winthrop. C. M.

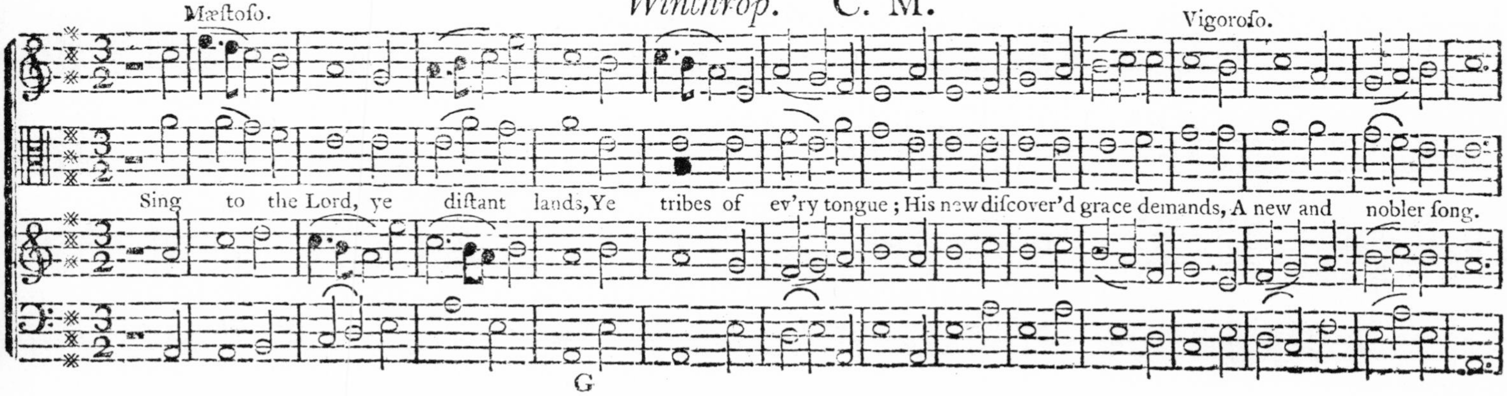
Mæſtoſo.
Vigoroſo.
Sing to the Lord, ye diſtant lands, Ye tribes of ev'ry tongue; His new diſcover'd grace demands, A new and nobler ſong.
G

Winthrop. Continued.

Say to the, &c.
Say to the, &c.
God's own almighty son ; His
Say, &c.
His pow'r the sinking
Say to the nations, Jesus reigns,
Say to the, &c.
And grace surrounds his throne.
world sustains,
His pow'r the sinking world sustains,
His pow'r, &c.

Union. C. M.

With thy, &c.
shall raise, shall
Our states, O Lord, with songs of praise, Shall in thy strength rejoice,
With thy salvation crown'd shall
With thy salvation crown'd, shall raise, shall
raise,
cheerful voice, to, &c.
raise, To heav'n their cheerful voice, their cheerful, cheerful, cheerful voice.
To heav'n their, &c.

An Anthem of Praise. Psalm 100th.

Andante.
Make a joyful noise, Make a joyful noise, Make a joyful noise unto the Lord,
all ye lands. Serve the Lord with gladness Serve the Lord with gladness : Come before his presence with singing.

Know ye that the Lord he is God, it is he that hath made us, and not we ourfelves: We are his people, and the
fheep of his pafture.
We are his people, &c.
We are his people, his people, we are his people and the fheep of his
We are his people, his people, his people, &c.
We are his people, his people, his people, &c.

Anthem. Continued.

Enter into his gates, enter into his gates, enter into his gates, &c.
pasture. Enter into his gates, enter into his gates, enter into his gates, with thanks-giv-ing, and
Enter into his gates, &c.
Enter into his gates, &c.
Piano.
into his courts with praise: And into his courts with praise: Be thankful un - to him, and bless his name. Be

Piano Duetto.
For Jehovah is full of goodneſs, and his mercy is everlaſting, For Je-
thankful unto him, and bleſs his name,
For Jehovah is full of goodneſs, and his mercy is ever-
hovah is full of goodneſs, and his mercy is ever, ever, ever - laſt - ing,
And his truth will endure to
laſting, For Jehovah is full of goodneſs, and his mercy is ever - laſt - ing.

Vigorofo.
Doxology. Divoto.
all generations, his truth will endure to all generations. Now unto the king eternal, im-

mortal, invifible, the only wife God, be honor and glory, honor and glory, honor and

Encore.
glory, Thro' Jefus Chrift, both now and ever, and ever, and ever, and ever amen.

Handfel. L. M.

Jefus fhall reign where e'er the fun, Does his fuc - ceffive journeys

Handfel. Continued.

run ; His kingdom ſtretch from ſhore to ſhore, 'Till moons ſhall wax and wane no more.

Gethſemane. L. M.

Divoto.

'Twas on that dark, that doleful night, When pow'rs of earth and hell a-

rose, Againſt the ſon of God's delight, And friends betray'd him to his foes.

St. Mark's. S. M.

And muſt theſe active limbs of
And muſt this body die, This mortal frame decay:
And muſt theſe active
And muſt theſe active limbs of mine Lie
And muſt theſe active limbs of mine Lie mould'ring in the

St. Mark's. Continued.

mine Lie mould'ring in the clay
limbs of mine Lie mould'ring in the clay, And muſt theſe active limbs of mine Lie mould'ring in the clay.
mould'ring in the clay,
clay, Lie mould'ring in the clay,

St. Luke's. C. M.

Return, O God of love return, Earth is a tireſome place; How long ſhall we, thy children, mourn, Our abſence from thy face.

Funeral Hymn. C. M.

Affetuoſo.

Why do we mourn de - parting friends, Or ſhake, at death's alarms Tis but the voice that Jeſus ſends, To call them
to his arms. To call them to his arms, T'is but the voice that Jeſus ſends, To call them to his arms.

Victory.
Andante.
The welcome news, Thro' ev'ry Angel's breaſt freſh raptures ſhall diffuſe. The day is come, When Satan with his pow'r ſhall
ſink to endleſs doom; No more ſhall we his hoſtile troops purſue, From cloud to cloud nor the long fight renew.

Spring.

The fcatt' - red clouds are fled at laft, The rain is gone, the
winter's paft, The lovely vernal flow'rs ap - pear, The feather'd choir, de -

Andante.
Pia.
light our ear.
Now in ſweetly penſive moan, coos the turtle dove alone.
Pianiſſimo.
Co - - os,
Moderato.
co - - os,
coos the turtle dove alone.
co - - os

Behold the hoſts of hell, How cruel is their hate; A -
gainſt my life they riſe and join, Their fu - ry with de - ceit.

Ecſtacy. C. M.

Some ſeraph lend your heav'nly tongue, Some, &c.
Some ſeraph lend your heav'nly, heav'nly tongue, And
Some ſeraph lend your heav'nly tongue, Some ſeraph lend your heav'nly, heav'n - ly tongue,
Crefcendo.
Some ſeraph lend your heav'nly tongue, Some ſeraph lend your heav'nly tongue,
Dimin.
1
2
That I may raiſe, &c.
harps of golden ſtring: That I may raiſe a lofty ſong, that I may raiſe a lofty ſong, To our eternal King.
That I may raiſe, &c.
That, &c.

Potency. L. M.

'Twas from thy hand, my God, I came, A work of ſuch a cur'ous frame.
In me thy fearful wonders ſhine, And each pro - claims thy will divine.

An Anthem for Easter.

Angels roll the rock away, Den of death resign thy prey; See the Sav'our quit the tomb,
Crescendo.
Glowing with immortal bloom. Shout, shout ye seraphs, Gabr'el raise Fame's e - ternal trump of

Forte.
Pia.
praife, Let the earth's remoteft bound, Echo to the blifsful found.
Saints of
God lift up your eyes, See the conqu'rer fcale the fkies, Troops of angels on the road, Hail and

ſing, Hail and ſing, Hail and ſing, th'incarnate God. Heav'n unfolds its portals wide,
Matchleſs hero thro' them ride, King of glory mount thy throne, Boundleſs empire is thy own.

Hal-le - lu jah, halle - lujah, halle - lujah a - men.
Halle - lujah, halle - lujah, halle - lujah a - men and a - men. Halle-
Hallelujah, Halle-
Halle - lujah amen, Hallelujah, hallelujah, halle-
Halle - lujah, praise the Lord,
lujah, Halle - lujah, praise the Lord, Halle - lujah, Praise the Lord, a - men, and amen.
lujah, Halle - lujah, &c.
lujah, &c.

Plenitude. L. M.

Array'd in beauteous green, The hills and vallies ſhine ; And man and beaſt are fed, By providence di-
vine.
The harveſt bows his golden ears, The cop'ous ſeed of future years.
The harveſt, &c.
the harveſt bows, &c.
The harveſt bows his golden ears, the harveſt bows his golden ears, The cop'ous ſeed of future years.

Unity. P. M.

'Twas my beloved ſpoke, I knew his charming voice. I heard him ſay, Riſe up my love, My faireſt one awake, Awake and
come a - way. Riſe up my love, My faireſt one, awake, Awake and come away.

K

Emancipation. P. M.

Hail! everlafting fpring, Celeftial fountain hail! Thy ftreams falvation bring, Thy
waters never fail; Still they endure, And ftill they flow, For all our woe A fov'reign cure.

Bliss. C. M.

My thot's ferment these lower skies, And look within the vail ; There springs of endless pleasure rise, The waters never fail : There
Mæstoso.
There I behold, &c.
I behold with sweet delight, The blessed three in one, And strong affections fix my sight, On God's eternal Son.
There I behold, &c.

Funeral Anthem.

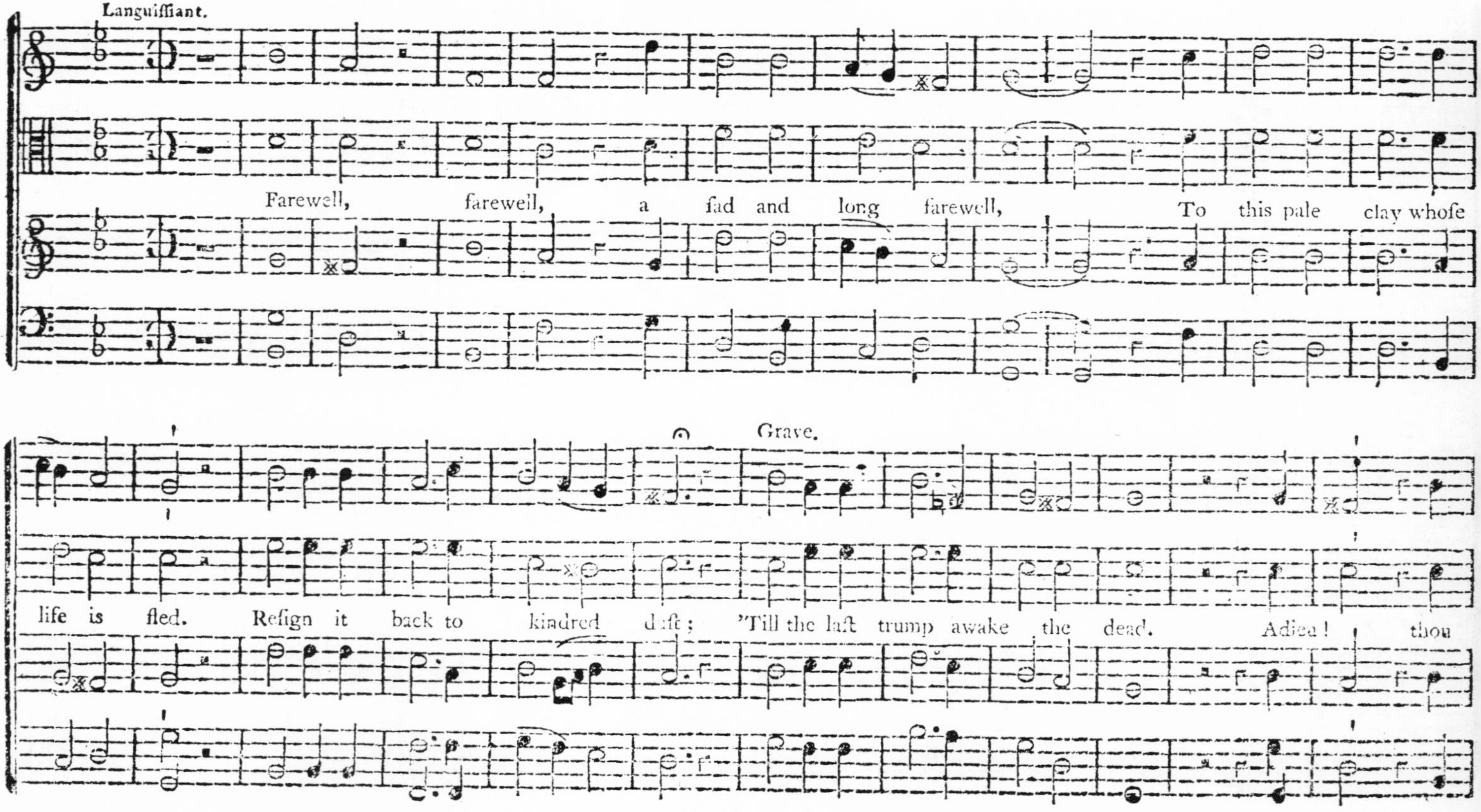
Languiſſiant.
Farewell, farewell, a ſad and long farewell, To this pale clay whoſe
life is fled. Reſign it back to kindred duſt; 'Till the laſt trump awake the dead. Adieu! thou
Grave.

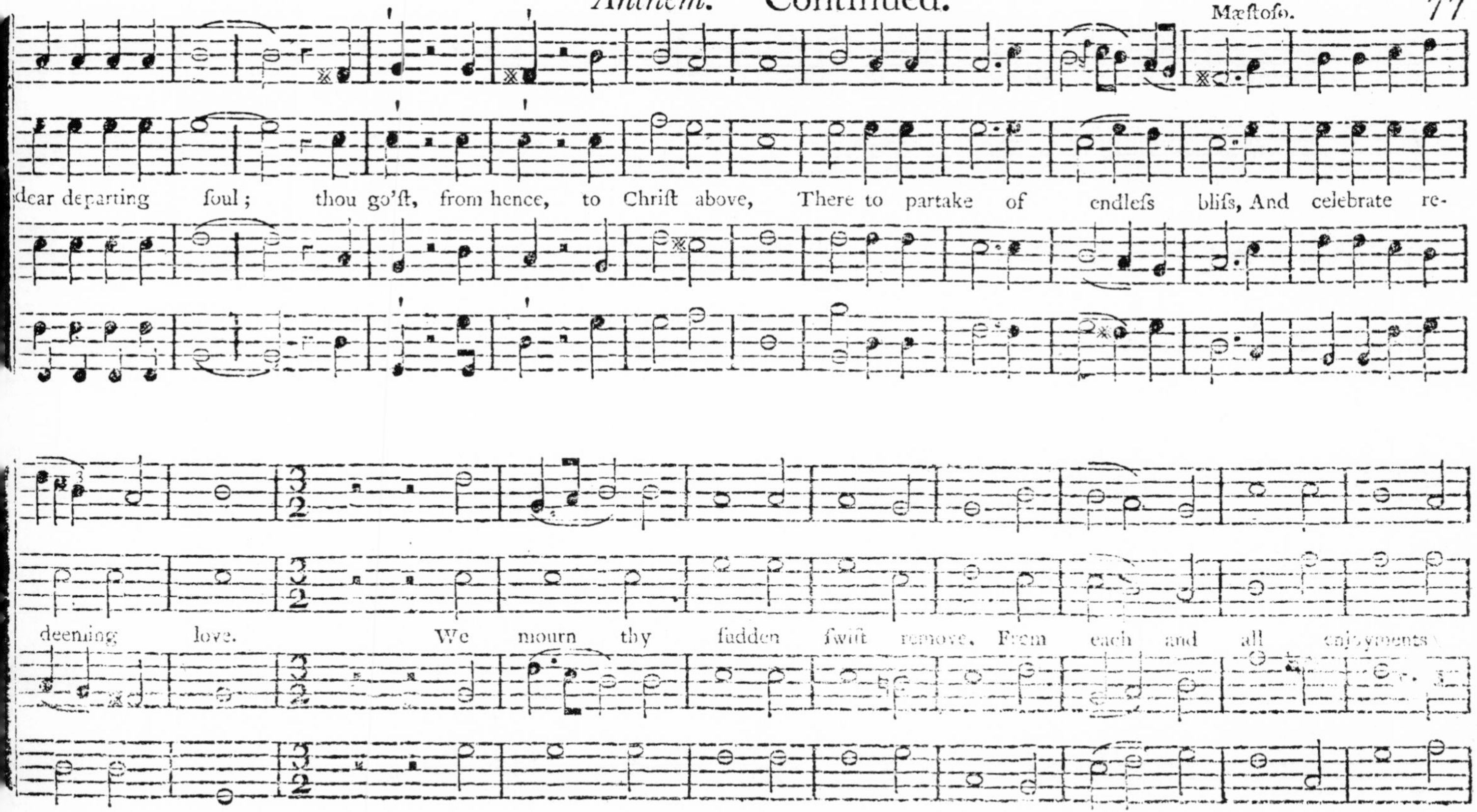
Mæſtoſo.
dear departing ſoul; thou go'ſt, from hence, to Chriſt above, There to partake of endleſs bliſs, And celebrate re-
deeming love. We mourn thy ſudden ſwift remove, From each and all enjoyments

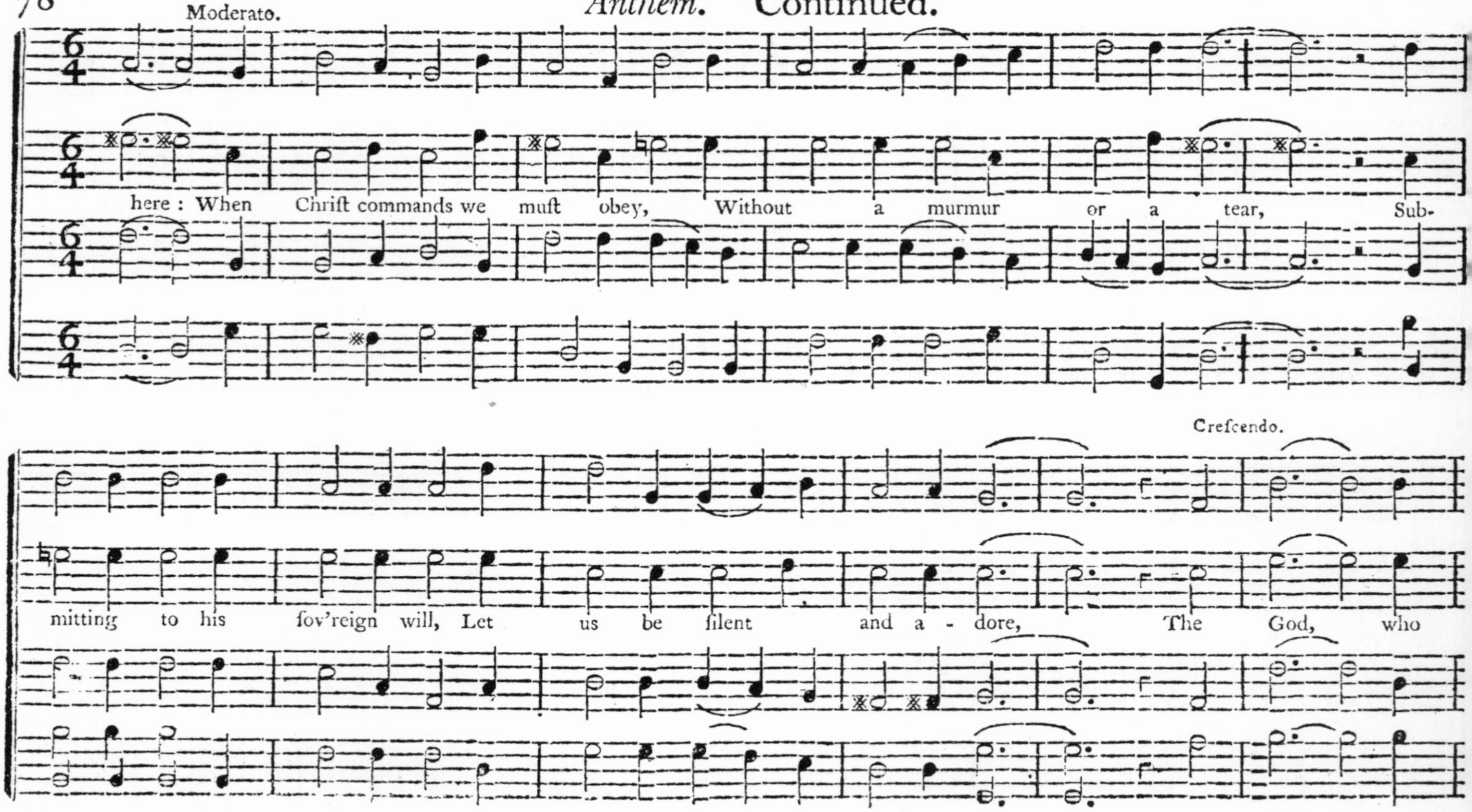
Moderato.
here : When Chrift commands we muft obey, Without a murmur or a tear, Sub-
Crefcendo.
mitting to his fov'reign will, Let us be filent and a - dore, The God, who

Anthem. Continued.

Diminuendo.
Grave.
hath created all, And all ſhall rule for ever more. For ever - more.

Sublimity. S. M.

Behold the lofty ſky, Declares its maker God, And all the ſtarry works on high, Proclaim his pow'r abroad.

Lamentation. C. M.

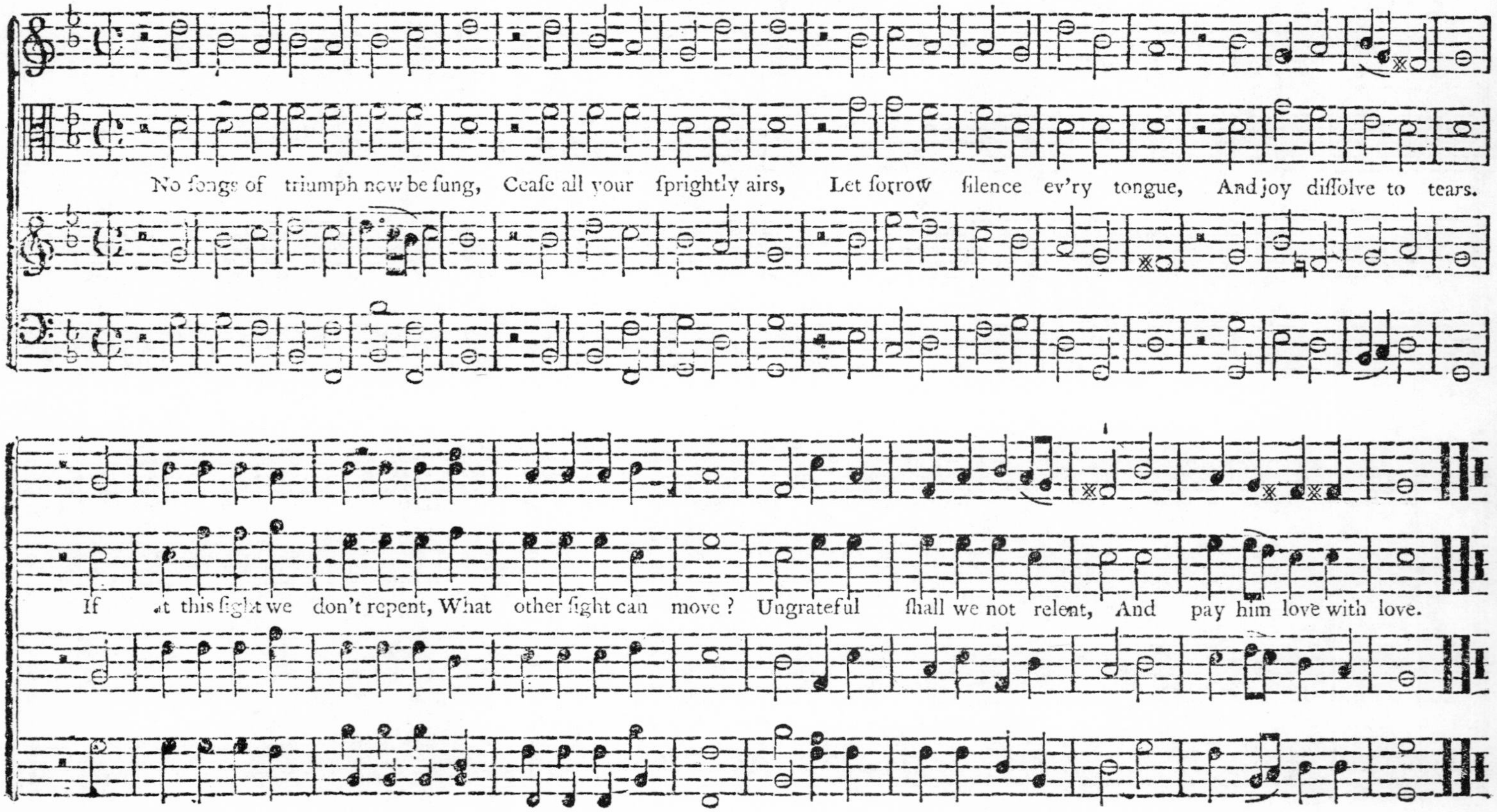
No ſongs of triumph now be ſung, Ceaſe all your ſprightly airs, Let ſorrow ſilence ev'ry tongue, And joy diſſolve to tears.
If at this ſight we don't repent, What other ſight can move? Ungrateful ſhall we not relent, And pay him love with love.

Sovereignty. P. M.

☞ This tune may be ſung as L. M. by ſlurring the three firſt crotchets in the laſt bar but one of each line.

All things from nothing, to their ſov'reign Lord, Obedient roſe, at
his commanding word, Fair in his eye the whole creation ſtood, He ſaw the building and pronounc'd it good.

New Sharon. L. M.

His, &c.
When fuch as we attempt to fing, The praifes of our heav'nly king, His mercies rife fo faft in view,
His, &c.
theme is ever ever new.
His, &c.
That ftill the theme is ever new, the theme is ever new.
His mercies rife fo faft in
His, &c.
theme, the theme is ever, ever new.
His mercies rife fo faft in view,

New Sharon. Continued.

view That ſtill the theme
His mercies riſe ſo faſt in view That ſtill the theme is ever new.
is ever new, &c.

Ocean. L. M.

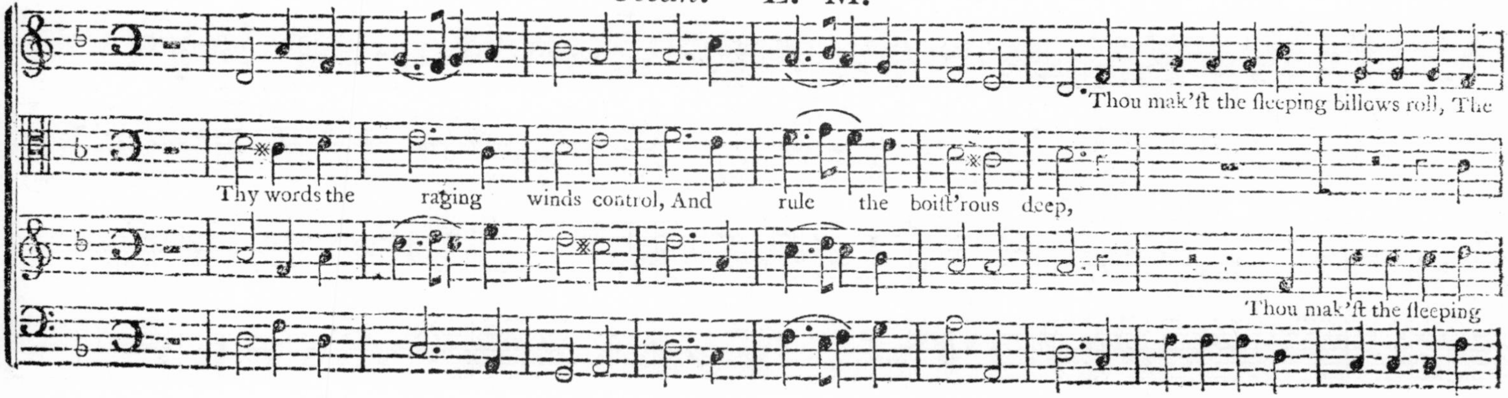
Thou mak'ſt the ſleeping billows roll, The
Thy words the raging winds control, And rule the boiſt'rous deep,
Thou mak'ſt the ſleeping

Ocean. Continued.

roll - - - - - ing billows ſleep, The roll - - - - ing, &c.
mak'ſt the ſleeping billows roll, the roll - - - - ing billows ſleep, the rolling billows ſleep.
billows roll, the roll - - - - ing billows ſleep, the roll - - ing, &c.
roll - - - ing billows ſleep, the roll - - - - ing roll - - ing, &c.

The Power of Muſick. Words by Stoddard.

Hark ! ſome ſoft ſwell, pants on the ev'ning breeze, The ocean ſmothes, and ſtills the

ruftling trees; 'Tis Pindar's harp, 'Tis Pindar's harp, in more than Pythian ftrain, Now ftrung to charm with fong each mental pain.
CHORUS.
Thus mufick's foft alarms can A'te's rage control.
And
And lull in dreams of ecftacy.

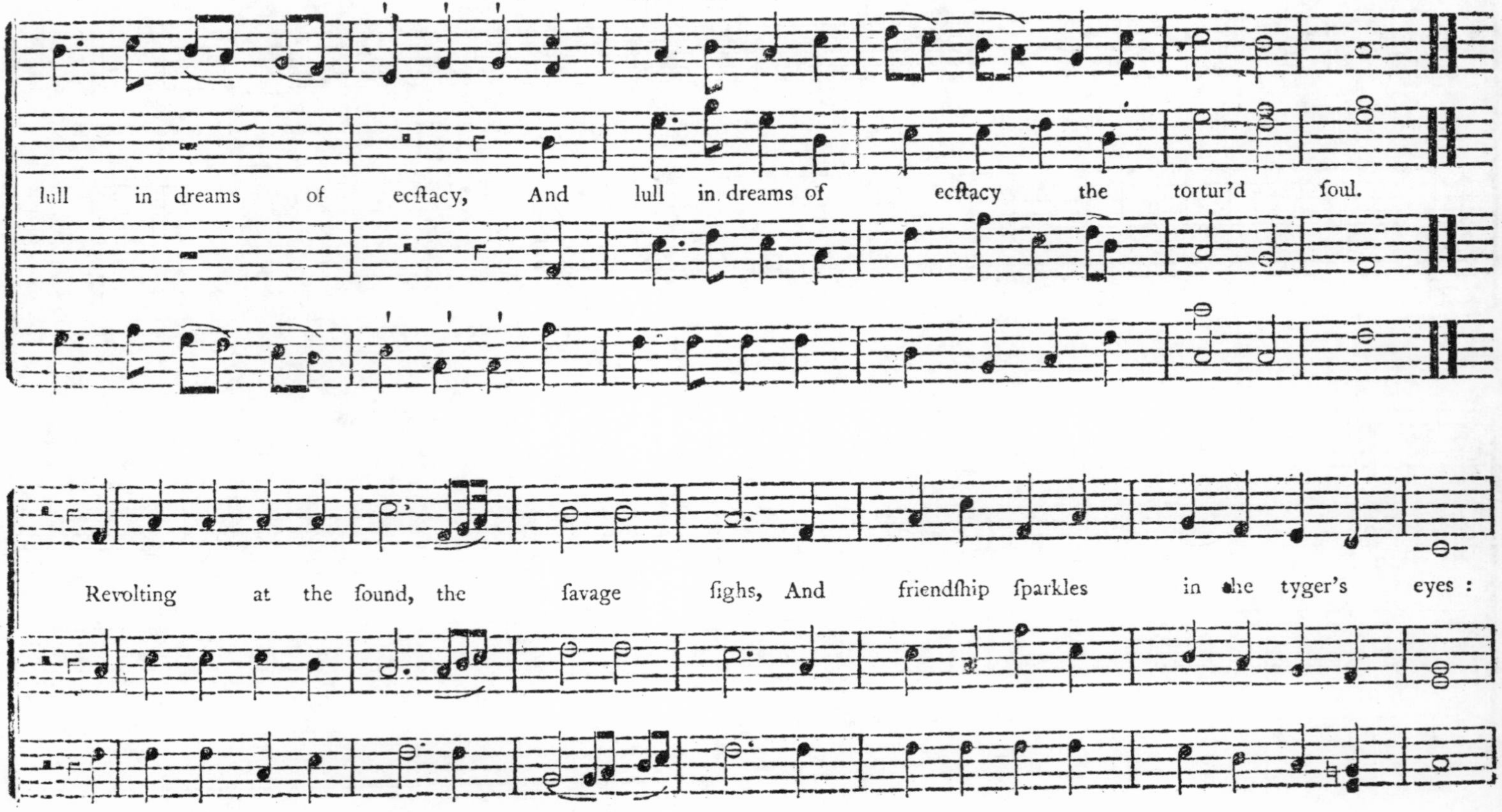
lull in dreams of ecſtacy, And lull in dreams of ecſtacy the tortur'd ſoul.
Revolting at the ſound, the ſavage ſighs, And friendſhip ſparkles in the tyger's eyes :

Lo! Jove's fierce bolts, in rapid flight expire, While hissing serpents drop their vengeful ire.

CHORUS.

Thus musick's soft alarms can A'te's rage control. And
And lull in dreams of ecstacy

lull in dreams of ecſtacy, And lull in dreams of ecſtacy the tortur'd ſoul.
Pale ſorrows die, alternate paſſions move, Awakes deſpair, or ſoftens into love; In

wild diforder haggard envy ftarts, And joy on fullen melancholy darts.
CHORUS. Mezza piano.
Piano.
Thus mufick's foft alarms can A'te's rage control.
And
And lull in dreams of ecftacy,

The Power of Muſic. Continued.

Pianiſſimo.
Creſcendo.
Diminuendo.
lull in dreams of ecſtacy, And lull in dreams of ecſtacy the tortur'd ſoul.

Reedfield. S. M.

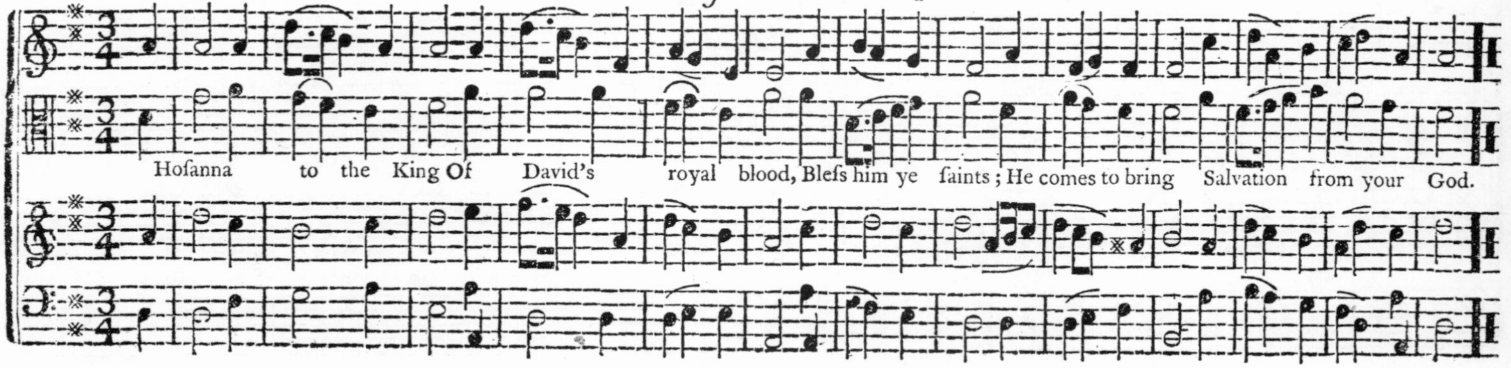
Hoſanna to the King Of David's royal blood, Bleſs him ye ſaints; He comes to bring Salvation from your God.

Turner. L. M.

Thy mercies Lord, ſhall be my ſong, My ſong on them ſhall ever dwell:
To ages yet unborn, my tongue Thy never failing truth ſhall tell.

Farmington. P. M.

Come my beloved haste away, Came my beloved haste away, haste, haste,
Come my beloved haste a - way, Come my beloved, haste,
Come, &c.
Come, &c.
Fly like a, &c.
haste away, Cut short the hours of thy delay; Fly like a youthful hart or roe, Over the hills where
Fly like, &c.
Fly like, &c.
Fly, &c.

Farmington. Continued.

Over the hills, &c. Fly, &c.
ſpices grow, Fly like a youthful hart or roe, Over the hills where ſpices grow.
Over, &c. Fly, &c.
Over the, &c. Fly, &c.

Sunday. C. M.

Creſcendo.
Moderato.
Dim.
Cres.
Ariſe, ariſe! the Lord aroſe, On this triumphant day; Your ſouls to piety diſcloſe, Ariſe to bleſs and pray.

Bath. P. M.

Not to our names, thou only juſt and true, Not to our worthleſs names is glory due : Thy pow'r and grace, thy truth and juſtice claim,
Immortal honors to thy ſov'reign name. Shine thro' the earth, from heav'n thy bleſt abode, Nor let the heathen ſay, and where's your God ?

St. John's. C. M.

With cheerful notes let all the earth, To heav'n their voices
raiſe. Let all inpir'd with godly mirth, Sing ſolemn hymns of praiſe.

Tranſmigration.

Come let us renew, Our journey purſue, Roll round with the year, Roll round with the year, And
never ſtand ſtill, Till our maſter appear. And never ſtand ſtill Till our maſter appear. His adorable will, Let us

gladly fulfil, And our talents improve, By the patience of hope, And the labour of love, The labour of love, By the
patience of hope, And the labour of love.
Our life is a dream, Our time as a ſtream Glides
N

ſwiftly away, Glides ſwiftly away, And the fugitive moment refuſes to ſtay: The
arrow is flown, The moment is gone, The millennial year, ruſhes on to our view, And eternity's here, eternity's here.

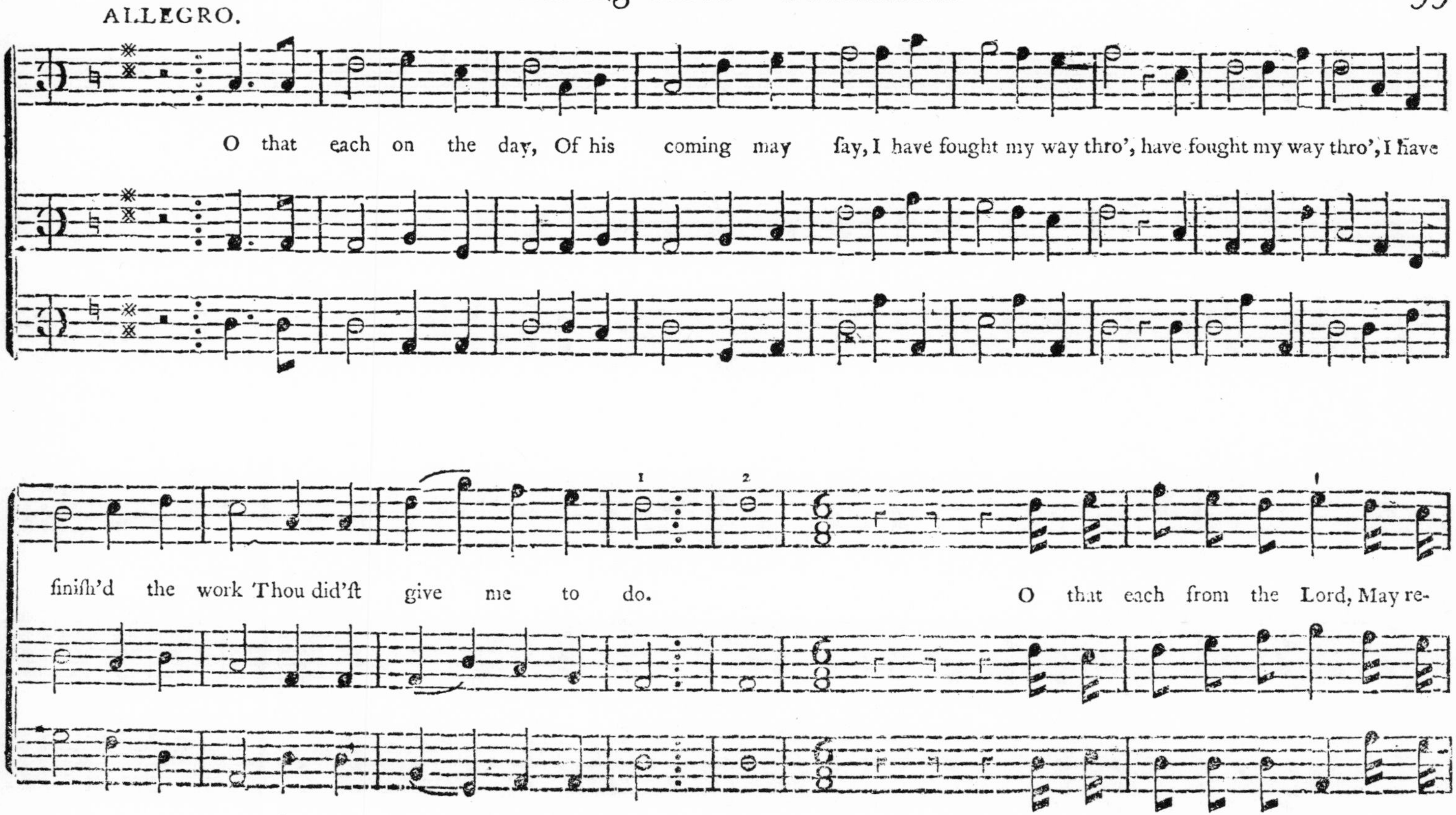
ALLEGRO.
O that each on the day, Of his coming may ſay, I have fought my way thro', have fought my way thro', I have
finiſh'd the work Thou did'ſt give me to do.
O that each from the Lord, May re-

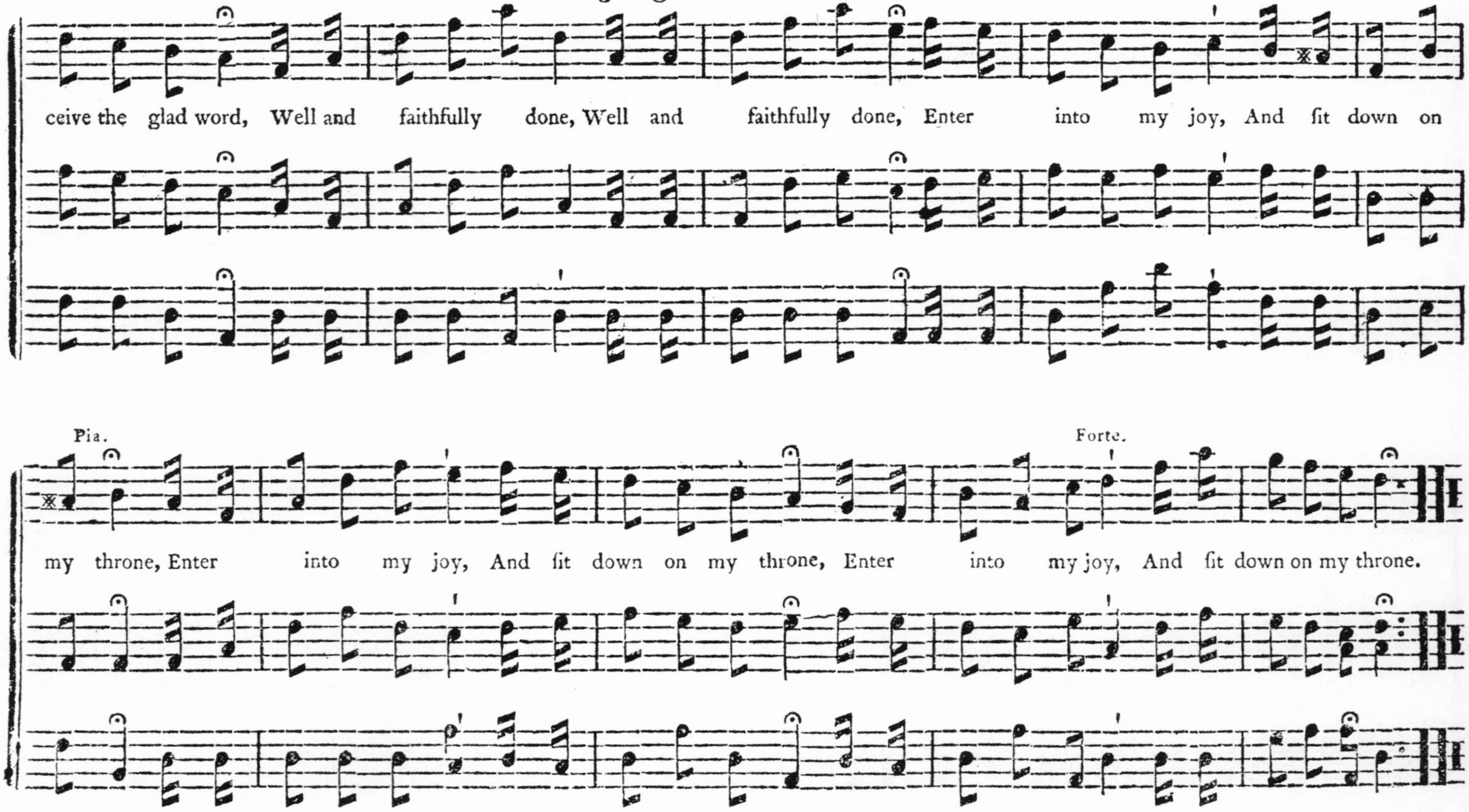
ceive the glad word, Well and faithfully done, Well and faithfully done, Enter into my joy, And ſit down on
Pia.
Forte.
my throne, Enter into my joy, And ſit down on my throne, Enter into my joy, And ſit down on my throne.

Captivity. L. M.

When we our weary limbs to reſt, Sat down by proud Lubrate's ſtream, We wept with doleful tho'ts oppreſs'd, And Zion was our mournful theme.
Our harps that when with joy we ſung, Were wont their tuneful notes to bear, With ſilent ſtrings neglected hung, On willow trees that wither'd there.

Cumberland. L. M.

He reigns ; the Lord the Saviour reigns! Praiſe him in evangelic ſtrains, Let the whole earth in ſongs rejoice, And diſtant iſlands join their voice.

York. L. M.

So let our lips and lives expreſs, The holy goſpel we profeſs ; So let our works and virtues ſhine, To prove the doctrine all divine.

Omega.

Presto.
Meaſtoſo.
Come thou Almighty king, Help us thy name to ſing, Help us to praiſe. Father all glorious, O'er all vic.
Pia.
Forte.
torious, Come and reign over us, Ancient of days. Come and reign over us, Ancient of days.

INDEX to the MUSICK.

ANTHEMS, &c.

ERRATA.—*Harmony*, 18th page, 2d bar from the cloſe, the pointed minim on G, in the Baſs, ſhould be on F.—*Hallowell*, 20th page, the laſt note in the 8th bar from the beginning, in the Tenor on G, a minim ſhould be a crotchet; likewiſe the 6th bar from the cloſe, in the 2d Tenor, there is one crotchet too many on F.—*Requeſt*, 34th page, the laſt note in the upper ſtave of the page, in the Treble, a ſemibreve on B, ſhould be on D; likewiſe in the 3d bar from the cloſe, in the 2d Treble, the crotchet on F, ſhould be a minim.—*Heroiſm*, 35th page, in the 4th bar from the cloſe, there is one crotchet wanting on B, the laſt note in the bar, Baſs.—*Plentitude*, 72d page, in the 10th bar from the beginning, in the Tenor, the third note in the bar, a quaver on E, ſhould be on F.—*New Sharon*, 83d page, 3d bar from the cloſe in the Tenor, the 2d note in the bar, a quaver on F, ſhould be on E.